W9-CLL-291

22,536

JK
271
.B639   Boskin
            Opposition
            politics : the
            anti-New Deal
            tradition

DATE DUE

JE 18 '91			
SE 20 '94			

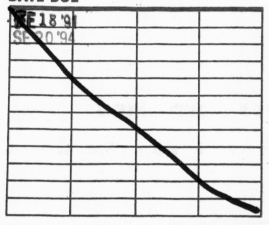

TICS:

dition

Opposition politics
JK271.B639   22536

Boskin, Joseph
    VRJC/WRIGHT LIBRARY

The Insight Series:

Studies in Contemporary Issues

from The Glencoe Press

Series Editors: Fred Krinsky and Joseph Boskin

Stanley S. Graham

OPPOSITION POLITICS:
the anti-new deal tradition

Joseph Boskin

Assistant Professor
Department of History
University of Southern California

THE GLENCOE PRESS
A Division of The Macmillan Company
Beverly Hills

~~VERNON REGIONAL~~
~~JUNIOR COLLEGE LIBRARY~~

Copyright © 1968 by the Glencoe Press, A Division of The Macmillan Company. *Printed in the United States of America.* All rights reserved. No part of this book may be reproduced or transmitted in any form or by any means, electronic or mechanical, including photocopying, recording, or by any information storage and retrieval system, without permission in writing from the Publisher. Collier-Macmillan Canada, Ltd., Toronto, Ontario. Library of Congress Catalog Card Number: 68-20277. *First Printing.*

Preface

This book deals with a most important feature of American politics: the opposition. It addresses itself to the following considerations:

    1) the nature and role of the opposition in relation to the party in power; and

    2) the configuration of the groups which have opposed the domestic programs of the Democratic Administrations of Presidents Franklin D. Roosevelt, Harry S. Truman, John F. Kennedy, and Lyndon B. Johnson.

Although the opposition to the incumbent party has not been institutionalized here as it has been in Great Britain, there have always existed individualuals and groups who oppose the policies of the Administration. Frequently the opposition has emanated from one of our two major parties; however, interest blocs, third party movements, and small groups have separately and at times jointly fought political programs. The first chapter of this book, entitled "The Landscape of American Opposition Politics," examines the various aspects of the functions, objectives and patterns of opposition.

The most influential contemporary voice of opposition has come in response to the New Deal programs initiated by President Franklin D. Roosevelt. Opposition to the New Deal on the part of many individuals and groups developed quickly after the first Hundred Days of Roosevelt's Administration in 1933. It continued to grow as the New Deal instituted many far-reaching legislative measures. Republicans, conservative Democrats, Socialists, Communists, Townsendites, Coughlinites, "Share-the-Wealth" followers, radicals of all types criticized the New Deal and called for its revision.

Because of the effectiveness of the New Deal in restoring and reforming the productivity of the American social and economic system after the collapse of the stock market and the Great Depression which followed, and because of the confidence it renewed in farmers, laborers, white collar workers, minority groups, urban dwellers, the unemployed, and millions more, the New Deal program was highly acceptable to the electorate. The administrations which have succeeded Roosevelt through the 1960's have maintained and expanded the basic framework of his domestic policy.

At the same time, however, the New Deal continued to engender more opposition. It appears that the more successful the New Deal policies the more vitriolic the opposition forces. A culmination of opposition was accomplished with the nomination of Senator Barry Goldwater of Arizona in 1964 by the conservatives of the Republican Party. Senator Goldwater was committed to repealing or drastically revising the liberal policies of both the Democratic Administrations since the 1930's and Republican President Eisenhower's "Dynamic Conservatism" as well. The character of the groups and

programs which have opposed the liberal policies since the 1930's has established what might be termed the "anti-New Deal tradition." This book uses
the concept of opposition as an insight into this tradition and contemporary
American politics as a whole.

J. B.

Los Angeles, California
November, 1967

(NOTE. — Throughout this book, the author–editor's footnotes are marked by
symbols — *, † — and the original quoted notes by numerals.)

Contents

Chapter One

Introduction: The Landscape of American Opposition Parties

One of the most durable, flexible and controversial of American institutions is the political party. Alternately attacked for its seeming vacuousness of ideological purpose and praised for its ability to hold dissident groups together, the political party in the United States is one of the most reflective mirrors of the social and economic scene.

This book is concerned with one of the least understood but most important factors in American politics — the groups that are not in power. What is the role of an opposition party in a two-party system? What is its function? What are the responsibilities of an opposition party in the American political structure?

The nature and role of an opposition party in the United States has been given little attention. Occasionally the word "opposition" is used by the mass media or by members of the party out of power but it is a word bereft of institutional meaning. For in the chemistry of the American political scene, the opposition has never truly been defined or analyzed. Moreover, unlike its counterpart in various European countries, the opposition party has no official political title and little institutional status. In Great Britain, for example, the opposition party has attained status and deference. The leader of the minority party is accorded the title "Leader of the Opposition to Her Majesty's Government" and his salary is paid by the state. Parties in France and Italy are not officially designated as belonging to an opposition, but they often differ radically from the program sponsored by the government.

Whether we label it as such or not, however, there exists at all times in the United States a group or groups acting in opposition to the party in power. The main opposition group is customarily identified with the major party which has been defeated at the polls in the previous election. At the same time, however, other groups usually oppose the incumbent party on a number of issues, sometimes over a considerable number of years.

In contrast with European opposition parties, the two major American parties are in basic agreement on fundamental doctrines. Conflicts between the in-party and out-party usually involve questions of administrative procedure instead of reflecting diametrically opposing values. The struggle for power may become sharp but rarely do the parties develop cleavages that lead to severe disruption. The nonviolent transfer of power from one party to another immediately following a reversal at the polls is one of the hallmarks of American politics.

The major American parties are basically coalitions of interest groups, blocs of voters, local machines, and socioeconomic classes; they are influenced by a myriad of local, national and international events. Consequently, there is a lack of centralized national control of the parties; this lack is paralleled in Congress and sometimes on local levels, too.

Despite, yet in some ways because of, the decentralized nature of the political parties, there are more specialized groups within the American political spectrum which assume the role of the opposition. Frequently these groups act independently of one another, but on some occasions they form virtually new parties for particular elections, and nominate candidates for the presidency. The nature of the American opposition is thus remarkably fluid.

However fluid, the opposition reflects the force and continuity of several traditional patterns in American society. The nature of opposition has been conditioned by four significant aspects of national political history; first, the tradition of pluralism; second, the existence of a basic consensus; third, the formation of cleavages in the electorate; and fourth, the political necessity that parties campaign on national, not local, issues.

One of the earliest observers of the pluralist tradition in America was Alexis de Tocqueville, who noted in his classic work, *Democracy in America*, this nation's preoccupation with the formation of unofficial groups and associations. America was a nation of "joiners." The prevalence of voluntary associations which has persisted since before De Tocqueville's visit in the 1830's has made for an overlapping and competition of loyalties. Political opposition in America thus has generally taken the form of numerous dissident groups, outside the major political parties, rather than the European form of opposition. Across the Atlantic there has usually been a unified, identifiable party structure whose primary purpose is to oppose governmental policy. The pluralist tradition in the United States has promoted a scattered opposition and encouraged conflict from and among a variety of sources.

Just as pluralism has encouraged conflict, the willingness of the various American oppositional groups to abide with the rules of the game has established the cornerstone of consensus.* All opposition in America is conditioned by this basic consensus; even groups at the extremes of opinion must

---

* For further discussion of the relationship between consensus and pluralism, and other problems of politics in today's mass society, see *Democracy and Complexity: Who Governs the Governors?*, by Fred Krinsky—another Insight Series book.

be willing to play by the rules. The existence of a consensus thus tends to moderate the methods, if not always the goals, of American political action, and also tends to discourage the very existence of extremism. The need to unite on nationally acceptable issues in order to achieve political success is another hindrance to the possibility of success for radicals. American parties have had to construct truly national platforms, find candidates who have broad appeal, and avoid identifying with regional antagonisms, in order to achieve electoral power. Dissident groups know that their ultimate success depends upon their ability to win support across cultural and geographic boundaries.

Just as a long political tradition has largely determined the pattern of modern opposition in the United States, so has the pattern of opposition continued to condition the whole American political scene. Each factor, acting in turn, has reinforced the other, and acting together they have formed a uniquely American style of governing.

The reading selections with this introductory chapter are chosen to point up the nature and importance of the four traditional American patterns of political behavior that have most influenced the development of opposition politics. The superficially conflicting, but actually complementary, traditions of pluralism and consensus are dealt with in turn by two selections from a report of the Rockefeller Brothers Fund, entitled *The Power of the Democratic Idea*. Robert A. Dahl's piece, "Cleavage," employs the concepts of polarization and heterogeneity to explore the great fluidity of political alliances in American society. And finally Samuel Lubell discusses the importance of coalitions and national issues in determining the configuration of partisan power.

A Pluralistic Society*

. . . A society with a thoroughly democratic social order will be a "pluralistic society." Such a society is the opposite of a totalitarian or monolithic society. It contains and protects many religions, many philosophies, many ethnic groups, many different people trying different ideas in different ways. It is marked by the wide dispersion of power throughout its various sections and by the existence of autonomous centers of decision-making authority. It offers individuals a chance to vote for more than one party, to choose among municipal or state goverments that have different patterns, to change their jobs freely, and to join—or to refuse to join—many different groups.

* From pp. 34–36 in *The Power of the Democratic Idea*. Copyright © 1960 by the Rockefeller Brothers Fund, Inc. (As it appears in *Prospect for America* © 1961.) Reprinted by permission of Doubleday & Company, Inc.

In a pluralistic society, such groups have distinctive characteristics. They are independent of one another, autonomous and self-supporting, and are strong enough to resist pressure from the outside and to maintain their integrity when the struggle is severe. Moreover, on the contemporary scene, these groups are usually specialized groups—a farmers' cooperative, a professional association, a chamber of commerce—which do not represent all the manifold interests of the individuals who belong to them. They represent only a limited and selected set of these interests. The great boon conferred on its members by a society organized in this way is that it releases them from total dependence on any single human organization. They do not have to accept the unlimited authority of any group of men; they can turn from one organization to another for protection; they can spread their interests so that few defeats need to be final disasters.

But a pluralistic society provides more than freedom. It provides conditions in which the habit of compromise has a chance to develop and opportunities for reasonable and rewarding compromises are likely to flourish. In such a society the citizen has many different interests and associations; no center of power and interest embraces all the others; no single issue becomes so dominant that all other issues pile up around it. When an individual has many interests and belongs to many groups, he is unlikely to risk everything on a single issue, and he is likely to bring an external perspective to the struggles in which he engages. Some of his interests may overlap those of men and women who are among the innocent bystanders. Some even may be identical with those of members of the group directly opposed to his own. Wittingly or unwittingly, in consequence, he is likely to see things a little from the outside and to rehearse the larger social issue in an inner debate in his own mind.

Thus, conflicts in a pluralistic society are likely to be milder than those that arise in societies in which the individual is wholly encased within the group to which he belongs. Specific clashes of interest are limited, and they occur within a network of intersecting loyalties. One of the most important reasons why compromise has been an effective instrument of American democracy is that American society has been pluralistic.

On the rapidly changing contemporary scene, attention must be steadily focused on the conditions on which a pluralistic society depends. Relatively few individuals in any modern society can accomplish their purposes without the protection and support of powerful social groups. Accordingly, a democratic society must meet two imperatives. It must see to it that all its citizens have the opportunity to join groups that can protect and represent them; at the same time, however, it must see to it that none of these groups exercises monopolistic power over the individual.

In the contemporary world, the totalitarian state and monolithic political parties have been the most vivid examples of this danger. But the danger is present even in the absence of overt totalitarian commitments. As the social democratic parties of Western Europe seem now to agree, the state cannot be the only employer in the community; its power over the individual must be checked by the existence of other possible employers. Similarly, the individual must be protected against private employers by his union and by the state, and his rights must also be protected within his union by the action of the state or by other appropriate means.

The objective of a pluralistic society is to give the individual a wide variety of real and interesting alternatives among which he can choose. When men speak of a free society this is primarily what they mean.

Consensus in a Democratic Society*

American democracy faces the test of an era in which the pace and scope of change are unprecedented. Everywhere, and not least in the United States, habits of thought and patterns of behavior that represent the inheritance of centuries are rapidly losing or have already lost their force. And in many parts of the world, aggressive ideologies have arisen which exercise a wide appeal. Leaning on democratic ideals at some points and subtly distorting them at others, they also challenge the democratic outlook in fundamental ways. If a democratic society is to sail through such storms and arrive successfully at destinations of its own choosing, it must possess inner forces of stability and cohesion on which it can call.

The first question we must therefore consider is the way in which the many groups and interests that compose a democratic society are held together. When a society concerts its efforts for the sake of common goals and when it does so without recourse to violence or terror, it counts on the existence of certain generally held beliefs, attitudes, and feelings. Let us begin by asking what kind of agreement a democracy may and must enforce.

---

* From "Consensus in a Democratic Society," in *The Power of the Democratic Idea*, pp. 17–26.

Allegiance to the Rules of the Game

The answer must begin with the recognition that democratic ideals have their origins in a variety of religious and secular traditions and that there is no single embracing philosophy which all citizens of a democracy can be expected to share. Experience shows that men can be equally loyal to democratic ideals even though they give different ultimate reasons for their loyalty. In the United States, Protestants, Catholics, Jews, and free thinkers have all found it possible to agree about the validity of democratic ideals. The practice of toleration that characterizes free societies is the hard-won product of bitter experience. As the religious wars of the sixteenth and seventeenth centuries and the ideological purges in contemporary totalitarian societies indicate, the effort to impose unity of belief in matters of religion and ultimate philosophy, far from unifying a society, can lead to extraordinary bloodshed and brutality and can breed hostilities which it can take centuries to erase.

Accordingly, there is no official creed—religious, philosophical, or scientific—that a democratic state can impose on its citizens. Each individual is free to try to win his fellows to his own views by every fair means. Truth in matters of religion, philosophy, or science cannot be determined by vote, popular pressure, or governmental fiat. The issues with which these fundamental human enterprises are concerned are too important to be regulated by political expediencies, real or alleged. In a democracy the state is neutral with regard to religion, philosophy, or science, and citizens are free to decide for themselves where they stand in relation to the ultimate questions concerning the nature of the universe and man's place within it. This is one reason why those who are deeply concerned about these matters are likely to prize democracy. Democracy does not ask them to conceal, compromise, or apologize for their views on issues so important that concealment, compromise, and apology are incompatible with honor and conscience. In short, cohesion is achieved in a democratic society in the first instance by carefully removing certain questions from the sphere of politics, by separating the things that are Caesar's from the things that are God's.

But if a democracy does not demand that all its citizens accept a common religion or view of the cosmos, what is the nature of the agreement at which it must aim and which successful democracies have largely achieved? It consists in a shared allegiance to the rules by which social decisions are reached.

In a democratic society it is expected that men will hold different aims and ideas and that these aims and ideas will sometimes clash. If common policies are achieved and enforced in such a society and if citizens accept peaceably the defeat of their hopes in the public arena, the reason is that they believe it better in the long run to yield and fight another day rather than sacrifice the rules by which victory in such a struggle is determined. In a democracy the preservation of those rules normally takes priority over the achievement of any other social purpose. This is the heart of the democratic political ethic, and the allegiance of an individual to this ethic is the acid test of his allegiance to democracy.

Allegiance to the rules of the democratic competition is not pure ritualism. Written into the rules governing the democratic process are principles that provide for orderly change in the rules themselves. Moreover, the rules that define fair democratic competition are of at least two kinds. Some, like the electoral process or the right of freedom of assembly, are set forth in explicit laws. If governmental decisions are made in contravention of rules of this sort, they lack authority and do not carry a mandate that must be obeyed. Other rules of the democratic process, however, are matters not of legal procedure but of ethical principle. They cover matters too subtle and intricate to be spelled out in detail, but they are exemplified by such principles as honesty in stating the facts, a separation of a public official's public duties from his private interests, and refusal to impugn the loyalty of one's opponents in legitimate democratic competition. The success of the democratic process depends to a considerable extent on the degree to which citizens adhere to such unwritten rules. For unwritten moral assumptions affect the way that written rules are applied and the respect that men hold for these rules. If men think the rules of the game are mere rituals without an ethical substance behind them, they will look upon the rules as deceptions or as meaningless frivolities. When a democratic consensus is vigorous, therefore, loyalty to the rules of the game is loyalty to the inner spirit as well as the external forms of democracy.

Formation of a
Democracy's Working Consensus

A minimal agreement to abide by the rules of the democratic process is not enough, however, to produce effective and resolute government in a democracy. Free discussion will yield no practical results unless men talk directly to each other, unless they address themselves to common problems and share some common assumptions; disagreements and conflicts of interest cannot terminate in agreements that men accept voluntarily unless they find a common ground on which to negotiate. In addition to generally shared allegiance to the rules of the game, democracy also requires a practical working consensus about definite issues.

What is this "working consensus"? In any stable democracy that has the power to get ahead with its business, a body of opinion and principle tends to grow up and to be widely shared. Men are not forced or legislated into such a consensus, and no one in a democracy can be required to accept it. But habit, sentiment, common experience, and the appropriate social conditions all contrive to produce it. And if it does not exist, even common allegiance to the rules of the game is jeopardized.

The working consensus serves to define the issues that must be solved and the effective limits of the political dialogue at any given time. Disagreements, often fundamental ones, arise within it; and citizens who stand outside the prevailing consensus often make precious contributions to democracy precisely because they do so. Nevertheless, when such an informal working agreement exists it serves to define what is and what is not a significant matter for public debate; and in a successful democracy such a consensus usually does exist. Thus, there may be controversy today about the priority that should be given to slum clearance in comparison with other projects, but there is now no debate about whether the elimination of slums falls within the area of the public interest. In short, the decisions that are made in a democracy, the compromises that are reached, and the actions that are taken are made in an environing moral and intellectual atmosphere.

The Role of Compromise

How is this working consensus achieved? To a large extent it is achieved by compromise, which is the workaday instrument of practical democracy. In the best of worlds men have different interests, and since resources are scarce, no individual, no matter how admirable his purposes, can do everything he pleases. The effort of a democracy is to arrive at arrangements that will convince most men that their interests have been taken at least partly into account. Democracy thus depends on the ability of its citizens to negotiate peacefully with each other, to give as well as receive, and to arrive at understandings to which they will mutually adhere. Such understandings form the point of departure for the next round of the democratic debate.

Far from representing a lapse from principle, compromise thus represents one of democracy's most signal achievements. Compromise is incompatible with an unbending commitment to an abstract ideology; but it does not imply weak wills or fuzzy minds. Groups within a democracy may and do struggle hard for the achievement of their purposes; and if they do not achieve their full program at any given moment, they can continue to struggle until they do. The ethic of compromise does not call for them to abandon the struggle for their ultimate purposes. It calls for them only to carry on their fight at all times within the rules of the democratic process. They will use the courts, the press, peaceful public demonstrations, strikes, and elections; they will not use violence, slander, personal threats, or bribes. A notable example from the past of this sort of resolute struggle was the campaign for legislation against child labor. A current example, remarkable for its courage, restraint, and respect for democratic procedures, is the campaign American Negroes are waging for full citizenship.

Focusing the Public Interest

The striking of bargains between different interest groups is only part of what is involved, however, in the formation of an enlightened democratic consensus. Contemporary American society is a complex social order composed of many different groups with conflicting interests. But it is also an intricately coordinated society in which the actions of any group can ramify outward, affecting the welfare of great numbers of people and perhaps the security of the democratic process as a whole. When strong-minded groups take decisions, or when they struggle with other groups, the pressure on them to behave responsibly cannot come only from within the groups themselves. It must also come from the outside. Something we know as the public interest must be focused, expressed, and brought to bear on the contending parties.

To give the conception of the public interest specific content and to make it come alive in the day-to-day affairs of a democracy is the task of many agencies. The press, the churches, the universities, civic groups, eminent individuals, political parties, all play a part. They will often have different views about the true nature of the public interest, and none of them, in a democracy, will occupy a position as a privileged interpreter and spokesman for the common good. But there is one agency that has an unequivocal responsibility to protect the public interest and a special opportunity to make it come alive in a democracy's day-to-day existence. This is government—at all levels. Government cannot claim greater intellectual authority for its judgments than other institutions in democratic society. Within a constitutional framework, however, it has ultimate legal authority, and it has the greatest power to voice the public interest forcefully and to see that it is protected. A democratic government's task includes much more than appeasing and conciliating different groups. It includes the duty to remind citizens of the larger frame of reference within which they act and to embody and enforce the common purposes to which they must contribute.

In any society there are certain common interests which men must seek together because they cannot seek them separately. The concept of the public interest stands first and foremost for such common interests. At the most elementary level, these include certain common necessities such as a sound currency, protected natural resources, roads, schools, police, sanitation facilities, and instruments of communication. But at a higher level they include values and purposes to which a society, by tradition or by its deliberate decision, is committed. In a democratic society the preservation of the fundamental rights of the individual and of the democratic decision-making process is itself a supreme part of the public interest.

Among the more important matters that today fall within the range of the American public interest so defined is an economy that combines stability of the general price level and a low rate of unemployment with a high rate of growth of production; an adequate system of national defense; a well-conceived and supported foreign policy aimed at preserving the freedom of the American people and at using the power of the United States to work for a peaceful and productive international order; a vigorous program of research in the physical, biological, medical, and social sciences; the orderly renovation of our metropolitan areas; an educational system that draws out the potential excellences of each individual, while at the same time cultivating in the young the habits of democracy and producing the trained intelligence, general and specialized, on which a twentieth-century democracy must depend.

As this imposing but incomplete list suggests, the agenda of activities that must be matters of organized and official public concern at any particular moment is not inscribed for all eternity. Nor is it an agenda which is self-evident. The determination of what lies within the public interest is probably the fundamental task which each successive democratic government must undertake. Its achievement in conciliating and adjusting the opposing interests within a democracy is not complete unless government itself affirmatively represents the overriding public good that must also be taken into account. For a democratic government does not exist simply to please as many groups as possible. It is the trustee of fundamental and common concerns which can otherwise be smothered in the conflict between special interests.

Moreover, there is a second meaning of "the public interest" with which a democratic government must also be concerned. The classic image of "John Q. Public" waiting outside the door while the men inside the smoke-filled room are plotting or quarreling catches this meaning exactly, although a little melodramatically. At times the idea of the public interest stands for interests that are likely to be forgotten, interests that are indirectly affected by an issue although not directly involved in it. To speak of a "public interest" in such contexts is to call attention to values that may be overlooked, to people who may be neglected, to damage that may be done because men are acting within too narrow a conception of their responsibilities.

While a democratic government is not the only agency that exists to bring such neglected interests to the fore, it is one of the principal instruments for doing so. It exists not only to represent interests that have already found themselves but to give a voice and shape to interests which without it would be silent and unformed. Government in a democracy, if it is good government, is more than a broker for those who have the power to bring their interests and opinions to its attention. It is a watchman against injustice and irresponsiblity, and a representative of those who need the helping power of government if their interests are to see the light of day.

Continuing Reconstruction
of the Democratic Consensus

The political leader cannot, by himself, create a conception of the public interest. He helps form, but he also leans on, the working democratic consensus. And the formation—or destruction—of this consensus is not an organized process. It goes on whether anyone wills it or not. Events take place and men respond to them, changing their beliefs about the kind of world in which they live and altering the judgments they pass on that world.

A little more than a century ago, for example, reports by Parliamentary commissions revealing conditions in British mines and factories provoked a revulsion of conscience in Great Britian that affected people in all classes and that fundamentally changed the context of political discussion and action. Thirty years ago, similarly, Americans clashed in their interpretation of unemployment. Some took it to be a sign of individual failure, others of an iron economic law. An overwhelming majority now believes that unemployment is a social ill which can and should be substantially moderated by government action.

In the long run few things are more important in the politics of a nation than such changes in the terms of debate and in the subjects around which discussion turns. This is why the mere presence of a consensus is not enough. Agreement about the wrong things can be immensely damaging. Nor does it suffice for a democracy merely to give answers to the questions it asks itself. It is important that it asks the right questions in the right terms and avoids wrestling with the ghosts of problems of a preceding era. While the preservation of the conditions that make for consensus must be the constant object of a democracy, it is not the preservation of the existing consensus in all its parts but rather the steady criticism of that consensus that should concern such a society.

In the end, a task that is indispensable to the politics of democracy is carried on outside the political arena. Scholars who conduct deliberate and detached inquiry into the facts, critics who attack encrusted habits of thought, moralists who glimpse new values of which their contemporaries ought to be aware, these and others contribute decisively to the course of democratic politics. Much that such men do may be misguided and wasted, and such success as their ideas achieve is usually achieved slowly. But the health of a democracy depends on its ability to sustain and respect those who disengage themselves from the currents of prevailing opinion. A democracy cannot stand a consensus from which there is no dissent.

Nor should the consensus that prevails be one that invites only apathetic assent. It is possible for a society to deal with its problems efficiently, to satisfy the private and practical interests of most of its members, and still to leave them unmoved and uneasy. Most men also desire something more from the societies they inhabit. They want a sense that large projects are under way and that they are part of some significant and enduring human enterprise. If their society does not give them such a sense, it is possible for them to be physically contented and yet morally indifferent or alienated. Totalitarian ideologies have exploited this demand, but they are not the best means by which this demand can be satisfied. A society that is moved by an image of what it can be and that translates this image into definite programs of action can also satisfy the human impulse to idealism.

Cleavage*

Robert A. Dahl

European (and American) observers have often underestimated the pervasiveness of conflict in American politics because political conflict in the United States does not follow the expected patterns of class and ideological politics. The American "working class" is obviously not arrayed against "the bourgeoisie." The sound of conflict is muffled by the outward consensus on ideology: everyone seems to be employing the same ideology, the same phrases, even the same words.

---

* From the section by Robert A. Dahl entitled "Cleavage," in *Political Oppositions in Western Democracies*, ed. by Robert A. Dahl (New Haven and London: Yale University Press, 1966), pp. 48, 53–59.

Nevertheless, an examination of cleavage patterns in American politics suggests three conclusions:

1) Certain types of questions or issues have been the subject of political conflict for relatively long periods of time.

2) These questions have led to extremely severe conflict about once every generation.

3) Ordinarily, however, the severity of political conflicts is greatly reduced by, among other things, the pattern of cleavage, which encourages conciliation rather than conflict.

The Persistent Subjects of Conflict

Dispute over specific, concrete policy questions tends to be of a rather short-run nature. The particular issues that provoke controversy in one decade are likely to be superseded in the next by other specific questions. Nevertheless, certain types of issues have been recurrent subjects of conflicts in American politics.

One of these is the nature and extent of democratic processes. This question has persistently reappeared in American politics in a multitude of forms. It was one of the basic cleavages of the Constitutional Convention itself, where a question at issue was whether the republic to be established under the new constitution was to be democratic or aristocratic in character.

.   .   .   .

Whoever supposes . . . that American politics has been nothing more than a moving consensus, a sort of national Rotary Club luncheon, has not sufficiently reflected on the recurrence of intense conflict, crisis, and violence in American history.

The Pattern of Cleavage

If cleavages have been persistent, and if at times they have led to intense conflicts, why, one might inquire, has the system not been disrupted more often? Why have American oppositions been, on the whole, so moderate? Why don't oppositions "debate the great issues" and "present clear-cut alternatives," as critics so often demand? Why is it that "opposition" and "government" are often so hard to distinguish from one another?

One reason was discussed in the preceding section: the ambience of consensus in which government and oppositions operate. As long as oppositions employ substantially the same ideology and accept much the same set of values as the administration, it is difficult for them to force debate on the great issues (for there are no great issues) or to present clear-cut alternatives (for alternatives clearly outside the common ideology are excluded).

A second reason . . . is the structure of government and politics in the United States.

But a third reason is to be found in the very patterns of cleavage that lead to conflict. Even though, as we have seen, Americans divide quite often on questions of democratic rights and privileges, on the place of Negroes in American life, and on the economic role of the government, and divide somewhat less often on foreign policy, these and other issues do not ordinarily divide them into exclusive camps. For two reasons, it seems, American politics is almost never highly polarized.

1) Differences in political attitudes and actions are not highly related to differences in socioeconomic characteristics—region, status, occupation, etc. Even though there is some relationship, it is usually weak: people in the same regions, or the same status groups, or the same broad occupational categories do not form distinct, homogeneous clusters of attitudes. Consequently, polarization of politics along socioeconomic lines is inhibited.

2) Differences in political attitudes and loyalties are not highly interrelated among themselves. That is, persons who hold the same attitudes on one question frequently hold different attitudes on other questions. To overstate the point, every ally is sometimes an enemy and every enemy is sometimes an ally. Thus polarization of politics along ideological lines is inhibited.

As to the first explanation, it is difficult to find any distinctive and persistent clusters of attitudes in different regions of the United States, except on the question of the Negro. Regional differences in political attitudes do, of course, exist; but the differences are, on the whole, weak. Southerners are not, for example, more conservative about the economic role of the government than people in other regions. In fact, on the basis of 1956 survey evidence, V. O. Key suggested that "on some questions the South turns out to be a shade more 'liberal' than other regions." Key also pointed out, incidentally, that "even with respect to the Negro the unity of the South varies from aspect to aspect of race policy. Southerners take a far stronger position on school segregation than on such questions as the protection of the economic rights of Negroes."[1] Nor, despite its reputation, has the Midwest remained (assuming that it once was) notably more isolationist or less internationalist than the rest of the country.[2] The reputation of the Midwest was created in part by its representatives in Congress, of whom a larger percentage opposed foreign aid in the period before and after World War II than among the representatives from other regions. Yet much of this congressional isolationism was more closely related to party than to region: Democratic congressmen from the Midwest have been, unlike their Republican colleagues, predominantly internationalist.[3]

Relationships are often found between political attitudes and various indices of occupation, socioeconomic status, and class. But strong relationships are rare, and often they are surprisingly weak. Thus in 1956 percentages of persons who ranked high on a scale of internationalism did not seem to vary a great deal according to whether the occupations were white-collar, blue-collar, or farming.[4] As in other countries, however, manual workers tend to diverge from nonmanual workers in their views on the proper economic policies of the government. The effects of class identification seem to be even greater than the effects of occupation; in 1956 a white-collar worker who identified himself as a member of the working classes was somewhat more likely to be in favor of government intervention in the economy on a variety of fronts than a blue-collar worker who identified himself as middle class. (See Table 1.) Yet because class identity is weak, manual workers do not differ as sharply from nonmanual workers in their voting for candidates and parties as they do in a number of countries. Among the major English-speaking democracies, class voting seems to be lower in the United States than in Britain and Australia (though higher than in Canada).

---

[1] Vladimir O. Key, *Public Opinion and American Democracy* (New York: Alfred A. Knopf, Inc., 1961), pp. 102–03.

[2] On a scale of "internationalism," the percentages in each region which ranked high in 1956 were 53 per cent in the Midwest, compared with 59 per cent in the Northeast, 58 per cent in the Far West, and 56 per cent in the South. Key, *Public Opinion and American Democracy*, p. 107.

[3] Leroy N. Rieselbach, "The Demography of the Congressional Vote on Foreign Aid, 1939–1958," *American Political Science Review*, LVIII (September 1964), 577–88, esp. 582–83.

[4] White-collar workers who identified themselves as middle class ranked a little higher in internationalism; otherwise, differences were negligible. See Key, *Public Opinion and American Democracy*, Table 6.11, p. 144.

*Table 1. Socioeconomic Status and Support for Stronger Economic
Role of Government*

Occupation of head of family	Class with which respondent identified himself	
	Working	*Middle*
White-collar	40%	22%
Blue-collar	50%	35%
Farm operator	41%	32%

NOTE. — Entries are percentages ranking high in support for government aid to cities and towns for building more schools; to Negroes for fair treatment in jobs and housing; in guaranteeing everyone a job; for medical care; and in providing electric power and housing.

Source: Key, *Public Opinion and American Democracy*, p. 143.

Ethnic and religious loyalties and identifications introduce heterogeneity into regions and status groups. The common belief that distinctive ethnic and religious identifications are weakening in the United States as the descendants of the various immigrants become assimilated into American life has been recently challenged in a study of ethnic groups in New York; the authors conclude:

> Religion and race seem to define the major groups into which American society is evolving as the specifically national aspect of ethnicity [i.e., the specific nation from which one's ancestors came — R.D.] declines. In our large American cities, four major groups emerge: Catholics, Jews, white Protestants, and Negroes.[5]

Yet, like region, status, occupation, and economic position, ethnic and religious loyalties do not as such produce sharp political cleavages. Voting patterns are very much more distinctive than political attitudes. Jews and Catholics vote more heavily Democratic than Protestants; Negroes vote more heavily Democratic than whites; and voters of Irish, Italian, Polish, German, and Scandinavian descent often seem to have somewhat distinctive voting patterns. The differences may be more apparent in local elections than in national elections, and most distinctive when a representative of their own ethnic group—or an enemy of their ethnic group—has a leading place on one ticket.

The extent to which religious differences cut across class differences is revealed in a very general way by the data in Tables 2 and 3. In national elections over the past generation, among both manual workers

---

[5] Nathan Glazer and Daniel Patrick Moynihan, *Beyond the Melting Pot* (Cambridge, Mass.: M.I.T. Press and Harvard University Press, 1963), p. 314.

and nonmanual workers, Catholics have voted Democratic in considerably higher proportions than Protestants (Table 2). The discrepancy was greatest between middle-class (nonmanual) Catholics and Protestants; many Catholics who had moved into nonmanual occupations maintained their traditional loyalties as Democratic voters. The differences between Catholics and Protestants were smallest in the elections of 1952 and 1956, when General Eisenhower was the Republican candidate, and, as might be expected, greatest in 1960 when John F. Kennedy, a Catholic, was the Democratic candidate.

Table 2. Religious Voting by Occupational Categories, 1936–1960 (non-Southern whites only): 7 Presidential, 2 Congressional Elections

Religious voting: % Catholics voting Democratic
minus % Protestants voting Democratic

	Manual workers	Nonmanual	Farmers
High	41% (1960)	59% (1960)	39% (1956)
Median	20% ('52, '54)	28% (1956)	14% (1958)
Low	16% (1956)	17% (1952)	− 5% (1954)

Source: Data taken from Table II, pp. 92–94, in Seymour M. Lipset, "Religion and Politics in the American Past and Present," in Robert Lee and Martin Marty, eds., *Religion and Social Conflict* (New York: Oxford University Press, 1964).

To look at the same data in another way (Table 3), Protestants split most sharply along class lines in 1936 in the midst of the Great Depression, when Franklin Roosevelt was running for a second term. Catholics split most sharply in 1952 when many middle-class Catholics succumbed to the appeal of Eisenhower; in 1960, on the other hand, Kennedy all but obliterated the appeal of class among Catholics by his appeal as a fellow Catholic.

Table 3. Class Voting by Catholics and Protestants, 1936–1960 (non-Southern whites only): 7 Presidential, 2 Congressional Elections

Class voting: % manual workers voting Democratic
minus % nonmanual voting Democratic

	Catholics	Protestants
High	28% (1952)	29% (1936)
Median	16% (1948)	23% (1956)
Low	6% (1960)	18% (1954)

Source: See Table 2.

Thus religion or ethnic identity may either amplify the effects of class and status on voting, as in the case of Negroes or working-class Catholics; or, conversely, religion or ethnic identity may depress the significance of class and status by providing a crosscutting cleavage, as in the case of middle-class Catholics and Jews or white working-class Protestants. Moreover, just as the impact of occupation and economic position on voting may vary depending on the state of the economy, so the impact of religion and ethnic identity is not a constant but a varying factor depending on current issues and on the candidates themselves.

More important, differences in voting and partisan loyalties among ethnic and religious groups do not seem to reflect significant differences in ideology or attitudes about policy. This is not to say that there are *no* discernible differences in political predispositions and beliefs among the different groups. It has been conjectured that "the sympathy which Catholic doctrine has had for trade union objectives, as contrasted with the greater emphasis on individualism inherent in Protestantism may in some part explain why even non-union middle-class Catholics are more supportive of union rights in this country."[6] In New York City, it has been said, "what attracts Jews is liberalism, using the term to refer to the entire range of leftist positions, from the mildest to the most extreme."[7] The kind of Christian pacifism exemplified by Martin Luther King's strategy of nonviolence quite possibly could not have succeeded with any other group of Americans as well as it did with Negroes.

Nonetheless, differences in attitudes and beliefs often reflect other factors like education and economic position; or else the differences are highly specific and depend on some particular issue that impinges directly on the group, as in the case of Catholic views on governmental aid to parochial schools or the views of Negroes on civil rights. On the whole, when these factors are removed it is difficult to find much distinctiveness in the political attitudes of the various ethnic and religious groups.

In short, then, differences in political attitudes and actions are related to a number of different social and economic characteristics, but they are not highly related to any, and the variety of social and economic

---

[6] Seymour M. Lipset, "Religion and Politics," *The First New Nation* (New York: Basic Books, 1963), p. 113. Lipset cites the following finding. "Ohio's counties were segregated (for analytic purposes) into twenty different levels of urbanism, income, and rural farm, and in all twenty of these groups the more Catholic counties exceeded the least Catholic in their opposition to right-to-work" (i.e. anti-union) legislation in a 1958 referendum. See also John H. Fenton, *The Catholic Vote* (New Orleans: Hauser Press, 1960), pp. 37–38.

[7] Nathan Glazer and Daniel P. Moynihan, *Beyond the Melting Pot* (Cambridge, Mass.: M.I.T. Press, 1963), p. 167.

characteristics of any broad category of the population makes for a high degree of political heterogeneity. Hence polarization along social and economic lines is inhibited.

The second factor mentioned a moment ago—that differences in political attitudes and loyalties are not highly interrelated—contributes further to this process. Despite the relatively low level of differences in political attitudes and actions among people in different regions, occupations, classes, religions, and ethnic groups, it is conceivable that Americans might divide into two distinctive ideological blocs, each of which was internally a rather heterogeneous (though not random) mixture of socioeconomic groups. In a very rough way this might serve as a description of the Democratic and Republican Parties. The difficulty is, however, that until the present the ideological distinctiveness of these blocs has been blurred because even on major issues persons who hold the same attitudes on one question diverge on others. Two issues of great recent salience—integration and medical care—furnish illustrations. One might speculate that at least in the North economic liberals who would favor medical care would also be civil libertarians who would favor racial integration in the public schools; conversely, the prosegregationists might also be economic conservatives. Doubtless there is some tendency of this kind. The relations are, however, very shaky. In a 1956 sample, among Northerners who favored medical care about half also favored racial integration in the schools; but more than a third opposed it. Hence a Northern medical care coalition would, in the extreme case, lose a third of its support when it endorsed racial integration. Conversely, Northerners who opposed a federal medical care program were almost evenly divided on the question of racial integration; hence their coalition would (in principle) split wide open if it took any definite stand on the issue of segregation.

Unless attitudes are highly polarized, it is impossible to divide a population into two like-minded collections of people. No matter what criterion is used for dividing people, as long as there are only two categories or collections, then within each category there will be many conflicting views. Given the existence of a two-party system, it follows inevitably that, unless attitudes are highly polarized, each of the two parties can hope to win only by constructing an electoral coalition made up of people whose views coincide on some questions but diverge on others. This is exactly what happens most of the time in the United States. And as long as (1) political attitudes are not polarized and (2) only two major parties exist, there can be no escape from two parties each with heterogeneous followings.

VERNON REGIONAL
JUNIOR COLLEGE LIBRARY

Is the pattern I have been describing a recent one? It is difficult to say, for we have surveys and election studies only for the past quarter-century. Yet there is substantial reason for thinking that low polarization has been the usual condition of American politics, and that the reasons for low polarization have been about the same in the past as they are now: large socioeconomic groups have generally been heterogeneous in political attitudes, and persons who agree on one question disagree on others.

Presumably there have been historical fluctuations; the tide of polarization ebbs and flows. Polarization has probably risen to high points during each of the major crises described earlier, and then receded. But polarization is rarely high in American politics and, it would appear, never persistent.

The Drama of Unification*

Samuel Lubell

To be successful in judging the likely shape of political things to come, one needs a basic philosophy as to what American politics is all about. Some writers envision this drama in terms of personality—of the Kennedys and Rockefellers, Goldwater and Johnson, performing like so many actors on the ambition-revolving stage of political power.

Certainly "the man" has acquired new importance in the nuclear-bottomed and TV-wrapped world. "Personality in politics" has become a new form of packaging through which "the issues" are sharpened or glossed over. Still, I believe there is much more to American politics than a stagecraft that tends to reduce the ideals of self-government to the level of theater-going, to selecting plays which titillate our fancies, and to applauding personalities with whom we identify vicariously.

Other political writers have been convinced by their study of history that the drama of American politics consists of new variations in an endless struggle of "the people" against "privileged wealth." "Liberals" drive their intellects toward devising novel ways of achieving the equalitarian ideal of "one man, one vote, one dollar"; Goldwater conservatives, in counter-reaction, like to emphasize the importance of the concept of checks and balances by reiterating the slogan that "the United States is a Republic not a Democracy."

* From pp. 10–15 in *The Future of American Politics*, 3d edition, by Samuel Lubell. Copyright © 1951, 1952, 1956, 1965 by Samuel Lubell. Reprinted by permission of Harper & Row, Publishers.

But I doubt that the essential drama of American politics will be found in either the heroics of personality or a "right" against "left" conflict. The real drama, at least as I see it, lies in the constant struggle for national unification, in a ceaseless striving for "a more perfect union" made essential first by our continent-spanning expanse and later by the astonishing variety of peoples who were drawn to this country. The screws of internal adjustment have been tightened by the mounting burdens of leadership in a time-shortened world.

My basic faith, born perhaps from my own immigrant background, runs to the belief that in the long run the political future belongs to the forces of unification. Somehow, often in ways that are not readily perceived, the unifying forces eventually win out over the dividing, separatist influences.

Always, conflict and conciliation are the processes by which unification is achieved. To make sense of what often appears like mob-like confusion, I have learned to focus on two key concepts—nationalizing forces and coalition politics.

By "nationalizing forces," I have in mind those developments—economic, cultural, political, technological—which tend to impose their influences across the whole nation, overriding old sectional cleavages and differences of tradition. These nationalizing forces are the carriers of change which disrupt the present and shape the future. In thinking about politics I strive first to identify these forces, and then to measure their impact on the major voting elements in the nation. Nearly always, change strikes different voting groups in conflicting ways—promising new freedoms to some groups while threatening others with the loss of old liberties. Progress in unification can usually be gauged by the extent to which this clash is reconciled.

The needs of American unification require a quite different party system from what has developed among European nations. In this regard I depart from many political scientists who have been urging a more formal structuring of our party system, requiring each party to advance specific programs of action for which it will be held "responsible." This effort to model American politics on European concepts of "right" and "left" ignores the fact that on the whole our party system has met quite well the special unifying demands of our country.

My own study of American politics shows that the normal political condition in this country is not that of two evenly competing parties. Usually, we have one dominant majority party—currently the Democrats—whose main function is to serve as the arena in which the issues of the time are fought out.

To be able to fulfill this role, the majority party must be able to attract and hold in coalition sharply conflicting political elements—Negroes and Southerners, Catholics and anti-Catholics, even factory workers and their bosses. This mixture of clashing elements is bound together by some cementing interests, but it also threatens constantly to fly apart. The threat of defection and disunity operates as a constant pressure upon the leaders of the majority party to search out candidates and programs which will reconcile the conflicts and dissensions inside the coalition.

As long as the majority party succeeds in unifying its voting support, it remains in power. If it fails, it falls apart, permitting the minority party to take over, as happened with Eisenhower's triumph in 1952.

It follows that the key to the political warfare of any period of American history—past, present or future—will be found in the conflict that rages among the clashing voting elements who make up the majority coalition. Strategists of the minority party must be constantly on the prowl for appeals to those elements in the majority coalition which threaten to kick up political trouble.

This concept of the majority coalition as the arena for our age explains, I suspect, why my own election reporting and polling has differed so markedly from the traditional polling methods which seek to reduce all voter reaction to "yes" and "no" statistics that can be fed into computers.

.   .   .   .

But the American electorate is much more than a packaging of statistics, or an averaging out of census characteristics. More than any other single factor, voting is dominated by the continuity with the past, being truly like a river that rises in the past and empties into the future. The electorate feeds into this river not as individuals, but as members of one or more voting streams, each with its own distinctive flow, its own flotsam and jetsam of loyalty and hostility, its own sluggishness to some issues and liveliness to others.

These voting streams are the tributaries that make up the majority and minority coalitions. The channels in which they flow may have been shaped originally by the geographical contours of the country. In many Southern states the basic political cleavage remains between the tidewater "low country" and the hilly "back country."

Or these voting streams may have been grooved out by man-made differences, over economic interest or class, of race, religion or immigrant background, of cultural and educational outlook.

Viewed in these terms, the makeup of the majority coalition becomes a truly wondrous phenomenon to explore, to probe into and to fathom.

Each voting stream should be studied as the carrier of its own special conditioning, its own predispositions, and its own agitations. Holding a coalition together becomes less of a contest in political arithmetic, of merely adding together appeals for each group, than the art of bridging, stilling or suppressing the many different inner conflicts that are borne along within each voting group.

Every presidential election becomes a fresh testing of the coalition's vitality, of the cementing strength of the ties that bind together the coalition against the disrupting force of the dissensions that tug the coalition apart.

Each election, moreover, is likely to be dominated by a quite different central conflict from those in preceding elections, with the key to victory or defeat shifting to quite different elements in the coalition, reflecting their sensitivity to the issues of the hour.

Thus the 1952 context pitted New Deal loyalties and fears of economic depression against the accumulated grievances of twenty years of unbroken Democratic rule plus the angers and frustrations generated by the Korean War. By far the heaviest defections to Eisenhower came in the insurgent South and among isolationist-minded Democrats, many of them Catholics, who saw the attrition in Korea as a vindication of their opposition to our being drawn into World War II.

In 1960 "the plot" of the drama revolved around a test of the extent to which history had been rewritten. Would another Catholic aspirant to the White House repeat Al Smith's failure? Or would the economic appeals that Franklin Roosevelt had added to the Democratic Party prove strong enough, even after the defections to Eisenhower, to give John F. Kennedy that extra margin of votes which Smith had lacked?

By 1964 the main drama of the testing had shifted to the effort of extremist Republicans to ally their economic grievances with the racial angers of the white South into a new antigovernment coalition. One can speculate how different the outcome might have been if the clash of whites and blacks had been pressed in a period of economic adversity. With prosperity booming, the cohesive ties of the New Deal coalition were never stronger; even the force of racial anger could split only half of the South.

It is not mere chance that we should always find inside the majority coalition those voting elements which are acutely sensitive to the most pressing issues of the day, whatever that issue may be.

For the essential quality of the majority coalition is not its "liberalism" or "conservatism" but its timeliness. The elements in the coalition must be alive and responsive to the newer problems around which the unification of the nation spins.

During the post–Civil War era of Republican dominance, the drama of American unification coincided with the needs of continental expansion.

Chapter Two

Political Catalyst:
The Spirit of the New Deal

Certain events in history produce far-reaching changes. The 1929 stock market crash and the Great Depression were the major events which led to the formulation of the New Deal program by President Franklin D. Roosevelt. Both the collapse of the stock market and the wide spread Depression were unforeseen occurances. Although several warnings of the flaws in the foundation of the stock market were given by some observers of the economy, few realized the real extent of its weaknesses; in the same way, very few were alert to the possibility of a deep economic depression. Consequently, the country was ill-prepared psychologically, politically, or financially for the quick break down of the economic and political institutions which occurred as the Depression began to make itself felt across the country.

From 1929 to 1932 the effects of the Depression intensified. At its peak in 1932, fifteen million persons were unemployed and millions more were only partly employed; hundreds of thousands were homeless and tramping the roads seeking work or escape from dire economic circumstances; hunger protest marches and riots in cities and towns spread across the nation; farmers refused to bring their wares to market in certain areas in the Midwest and East and barricaded the roads; thousands of banks shut down because of bank "runs" and lack of funds; major demonstrations such as the Bonus March on the capitol in 1932 caused serious concern for the stability of the political system. By 1932 the country echoed with doubts that capitalism could survive; the mood of the nation was pessimistic and fearful.

The program of the New Deal emerged from President Roosevelt's attempt to cope with these complex national problems. Because of its sweep and depth, some have argued that the New Deal brought about a revolution in American society — which accounts for a considerable portion of the opposition it engendered. Within a few years after its inception the New Deal was actively opposed by a number of individuals and groups as well as by the Republican Party. In fact, the number of the groups which severely criticized Roosevelt and the New Deal was indicative of the changes which were being initiated by the Democratic Party.

The following selection from Professor William E. Leuchtenburg's book, *Franklin D. Roosevelt and the New Deal*, provides an excellent overview of these phenomena.

The Roosevelt Reconstruction: Retrospect*

William E. Leuchtenburg

In eight years [1932–1940], Roosevelt and the New Dealers had almost revolutionized the agenda of American politics. "Mr. Roosevelt may have given the wrong answers to many of his problems," concluded the editors of *The Economist*. "But he is at least the first President of modern America who has asked the right questions." In 1932, men of acumen were absorbed to an astonishing degree with such questions as prohibition, war debts, and law enforcement. By 1936, they were debating social security, the Wagner Act, valley authorities, and public housing. The thirties witnessed a rebirth of issues politics, and parties split more sharply on ideological lines than they had in many years past. "I incline to think that for years up to the present juncture thinking Democrats and thinking Republicans had been divided by an imaginary line," reflected a Massachusetts congressman in 1934. "Now for the first time since the period before the Civil War we find vital principles at stake." Much of this change resulted simply from the depression trauma, but much too came from the force of Roosevelt's personality and his use of his office as both pulpit and lectern. "Of course you have fallen into some errors—that is human," former Supreme Court Justice John Clarke wrote the President, "but you have put a new face upon the social and political life of our country."[1]

---

* From Chapter 14 by the same title, pp. 326–33, in *Franklin D. Roosevelt and the New Deal* by William E. Leuchtenburg. Copyright © 1963 by William E. Leuchtenburg. Reprinted by permission of Harper & Row, Publishers.

1 The Editors of the Economist, *The New Deal* (New York: 1937), p. 149; Representative Robert Luce to Herbert Claiborne Pell, November 14, 1934, Pell MSS., Box 7; Elliott Roosevelt (ed.), *F.D.R.: His Personal Letters, 1928-1945*, I (2 vols.; New York: 1950), 723.

Franklin Roosevelt re-created the modern presidency. He took an office which had lost much of its prestige and power in the previous twelve years and gave it an importance which went well beyond what even Theodore Roosevelt and Woodrow Wilson had done. Clinton Rossiter has observed: "Only Washington, who made the office, and Jackson, who remade it, did more than [Roosevelt] to raise it to its present condition of strength, dignity, and independence."[2] Under Roosevelt, the White House became the focus of all government—the fountainhead of ideas, the initiator of action, the representative of the national interest.

Roosevelt greatly expanded the president's legislative functions. In the nineteenth century, Congress had been jealous of its prerogatives as the lawmaking body, and resented any encroachment on its domain by the chief executive. Woodrow Wilson and Theodore Roosevelt had broken new ground in sending actual drafts of bills to Congress and in using devices like the caucus to win enactment of measures they favored. Franklin Roosevelt made such constant use of these tools that he came to assume a legislative role not unlike that of a prime minister. He sent special messages to Congress, accompanied them with drafts of legislation prepared by his assistants, wrote letters to committee chairmen or members of Congress to urge passage of the proposals, and authorized men like Corcoran to lobby as presidential spokesmen on the Hill. By the end of Roosevelt's tenure in the White House, Congress looked automatically to the Executive for guidance; it expected the administration to have a "program" to present for consideration.[3]

Roosevelt's most important formal contribution was his creation of the Executive Office of the President on September 8, 1939. Executive Order 8248, a "nearly unnoticed but none the less epoch-making event in the history of American institutions," set up an Executive Office staffed with six administrative assistants with a "passion for anonymity."[4] In 1939, the President not only placed obvious agencies like the White House Office in the Executive Office but made the crucial decision to shift the Bureau of the Budget from the Treasury and put it under his wing. In later years, such pivotal agencies as the Council of

---

[2] Clinton Rossiter, *The American Presidency* (New York: Signet, 1956), p. 114.

[3] *Ibid.*, pp. 81–84; Edward S. Corwin, *The President: Office and Powers 1787–1957* (New York: 1957), pp. 274–75. Yet despite the growth of the Presidency, this was a period in which Congress had great influence. Much of the specific New Deal legislation was the consequence of the work of a Robert Wagner or a Robert La Follette, Jr. The expansion of the Presidency resulted in a reinvigoration of the whole political system.

[4] Luther Gulick, cited in Rossiter, *The American Presidency*, p. 96.

Economic Advisors, the National Security Council, and the Central Intelligence Agency would be moved into the Executive Office of the President. Roosevelt's decision, Rossiter has concluded, "converts the Presidency into an instrument of twentieth-century government; it gives the incumbent a sporting chance to stand the strain and fulfill his constitutional mandate as a one-man branch of our three-part government; it deflates even the most forceful arguments, which are still raised occasionally, for a plural executive; it assures us that the Presidency will survive the advent of the positive state. Executive Order 8248 may yet be judged to have saved the Presidency from paralysis and the Constitution from radical amendment."[5]

Roosevelt's friends have been too quick to concede that he was a poor administrator. To be sure, he found it difficult to discharge incompetent aides, he procrastinated about decisions, and he ignored all the canons of sound administration by giving men overlapping assignments and creating a myriad of agencies which had no clear relation to the regular departments of government.[6] But if the test of good administration is not an impeccable organizational chart but creativity, then Roosevelt must be set down not merely as a good administrator but as a resourceful innovator. The new agencies he set up gave a spirit of excitement to Washington that the routinized old-line departments could never have achieved. The President's refusal to proceed through channels, however vexing at times to his subordinates, resulted in a competition not only among men but among ideas, and encouraged men to feel that their own beliefs might win the day. "You would be surprised, Colonel, the remarkable ideas that have been turned loose just because men have felt that they can get a hearing," one senator confided.[7] The President's "procrastination" was his own way both of arriving at a sense of national consensus and of reaching a decision by observing a trial by combat among rival theories. Periods of indecision —as in the spring of 1935 or the beginning of 1938—were inevitably followed by a fresh outburst of new proposals.[8]

---

[5] Rossiter, *American Presidency*, p. 100. Cf. Emile Giraud, *La Crise de la démocratie et le renforcement du pouvoir exécutif* (Paris: 1938).

[6] "At times Roosevelt acted as if a new agency were almost a new solution. His addiction to new organizations became a kind of nervous tic which disturbed even avid New Dealers." Arthur Schlesinger, Jr., *The Coming of the New Deal* (Boston: Houghton Mifflin Co., 1959), p. 535. Schlesinger has an excellent discussion of Roosevelt's administrative talent.

[7] Elbert Thomas to Colonel E. LeRoy Bourne, January 6, 1934, Elbert Thomas MSS., Box 23.

[8] Richard Neustadt, *Presidential Power* (New York: John Wiley & Sons, 1960), pp. 156–58.

Most of all, Roosevelt was a successful administrator because he attracted to Washington thousands of devoted and highly skilled men. Men who had been fighting for years for lost causes were given a chance: John Collier, whom the President courageously named Indian Commissioner; Arthur Powell Davis, who had been ousted as chief engineer of the Department of the Interior at the demand of power interests; old conservationists like Harry Slattery, who had fought the naval oil interests in the Harding era. When Harold Ickes took office as Secretary of the Interior, he looked up Louis Glavis—he did not even know whether the "martyr" of the Ballinger–Pinchot affair was still alive—and appointed him to his staff.[9]

The New Dealers displayed striking ingenuity in meeting problems of governing. They coaxed salmon to climb ladders at Bonneville; they sponsored a Young Choreographers Laboratory in the WPA's Dance Theatre; they gave the pioneer documentary film maker Pare Lorentz the opportunity to create his classic films *The Plow That Broke the Plains* and *The River*. At the Composers Forum–Laboratory of the Federal Music Project, William Schuman received his first serious hearing. In Arizona, Father Berard Haile of St. Michael's Mission taught written Navajo to the Indians.[10] Roosevelt, in the face of derision from professional foresters and prairie states' governors, persisted in a bold scheme to plant a mammoth "shelterbelt" of parallel rows of trees from the Dakotas to the Panhandle. In all, more than two hundred million trees were planted—cottonwood and willow, hackberry and cedar, Russian olive and Osage orange; within six years, the President's visionary windbreak had won over his former critics.[11] The spirit behind such innovations generated a new excitement about the potentialities of government. "Once again," Roosevelt told a group of young Democrats in April, 1936, "the very air of America is exhilarating."[12]

Roosevelt dominated the front pages of the newspapers as no other President before or since has done. "Frank Roosevelt and the NRA

---

[9] In Roosevelt's first year in office, he signed an order restoring Glavis to the civil service status he had lost when President Taft fired him. Ironically, Ickes found Glavis as intolerable a subordinate as Taft had, and concluded that he had "been very unjust to Ballinger all of these years." *The Secret Diary of Harold Ickes* (3 vols.; New York: 1954), III, p. 111.

[10] John Collier to Louis Brandeis, April 5, 1937, Brandeis MSS., SC 19.

[11] H. H. Chapman, "Digest of Opinions Received on the Shelterbelt Project," *Journal of Forestry*, XXXII (1934), 952–57; Bristow Adams, "Some Fence!" *Cornell Countryman*, XXXII (1934), 4; *Science News Letter*, CXXXIV (1938), 409; "Prairie Tree Banks," *American Forester*, CXLVII (1941), 177.

[12] Samuel Rosenman (ed.), *The Public Papers and Addresses of Franklin D. Roosevelt* (13 vols.; New York: 1938–50), V, p. 165.

have taken the place of love nests," commented Joe Patterson, publisher of the tabloid *New York Daily News*. At his very first conference, Roosevelt abolished the written question and told reporters they could interrogate him without warning. Skeptics predicted the free and easy exchange would soon be abandoned, but twice a week, year in and year out, he threw open the White House doors to as many as two hundred reporters, most of them representing hostile publishers, who would crowd right up to the President's desk to fire their questions. The President joshed them, traded wisecracks with them, called them by their first names; he charmed them by his good-humored ease and impressed them with his knowledge of detail.[13] To a degree, Roosevelt's press conference introduced, as some observers claimed, a new institution like Britain's parliamentary questioning; more to the point, it was a device the President manipulated, disarmingly and adroitly, to win support for his program.[14] It served too as a classroom to instruct the country in the new economics and the new politics.

Roosevelt was the first president to master the technique of reaching people directly over the radio. In his fireside chats, he talked like a father discussing public affairs with his family in the living room. As he spoke, he seemed unconscious of the fact that he was addressing millions. "His head would nod and his hands would move in simple, natural, comfortable gestures," Frances Perkins recalled. "His face would smile and light up as though he were actually sitting on the front porch or in the parlor with them." Eleanor Roosevelt later observed that after the President's death people would stop her on the street to say "they missed the way the President used to talk to them. They'd say 'He used to talk to me about my government.' There was a real dialogue between Franklin and the people," she reflected. "That dialogue seems to have disappeared from the government since he died."[15]

For the first time for many Americans, the federal government became an institution that was directly experienced. More than state and local governments, it came to "be *the* government, and agency directly

---

[13] Elmer Cornwell, Jr., "Presidential News: The Expanding Public Image," *Journalism Quarterly*, XXXVI (1959), 275–83; "The Chicago Tribune," *Fortune*, IX (May, 1934), 108; *Editor and Publisher* (March 4, 1933); Thomas Stokes, *Chip Off My Shoulder* (Princeton: 1940), p. 367.

[14] Erwin Canham, "Democracy's Fifth Wheel," *Literary Digest*, CXIX (January 5, 1935), 6; Douglass Cater, *The Fourth Branch of Government* (Boston: Houghton Mifflin Co., 1959), pp. 13–14, 142–55; James Pollard, *The Presidents and the Press* (New York: 1947), pp. 773–845.

[15] Frances Perkins, *The Roosevelt I Knew* (New York: 1946), p. 72; Bernard Asbéll, *When F.D.R. Died* (New York: 1961), p. 161.

concerned with their welfare. It was the source of their relief payments; it taxed them directly for old age pensions; it even gave their children hot lunches in school. As the role of the state changed from that of neutral arbiter to a "powerful promoter of society's welfare," people felt an interest in affairs in Washington they had never had before.[16]

Franklin Roosevelt personified the state as protector. It became commonplace to say that people felt toward the President the kind of trust they would normally express for a warm and understanding father who comforted them in their grief or safeguarded them from harm. An insurance man reported: "My mother looks upon the President as someone so immediately concerned with her problems and difficulties that she would not be greatly surprised were he to come to her house some evening and stay to dinner." From his first hours in office, Roosevelt gave people the feeling that they could confide in him directly. As late as the presidency of Herbert Hoover, one man, Ira Smith, had sufficed to take care of all the mail the White House received. Under Roosevelt, Smith had to acquire a staff of fifty people to handle the thousands of letters written to the President each week. Roosevelt gave people a sense of membership in the national community. Justice Douglas has written: "He was in a very special sense the people's President, because he made them feel that with him in the White House they shared the Presidency. The sense of sharing the Presidency gave even the most humble citizen a lively sense of belonging."[17]

When Roosevelt took office, the country, to a very large degree, responded to the will of a single element: the white, Anglo-Saxon, Protestant property-holding class. Under the New Deal, new groups took their place in the sun. It was not merely that they received benefits they had not had before but that they were "recognized" as having a place in the commonwealth. At the beginning of the Roosevelt era, charity organizations ignored labor when seeking "community" representation; at the end of the period, no fund-raising committee was complete without a union representative. While Theodore Roosevelt had founded a lily-white Progressive Party in the South and Woodrow Wilson had introduced segregation into the federal government, Franklin Roosevelt had quietly brought the Negro into the New Deal coalition. When the distinguished Negro contralto Marian Anderson was denied a concert hall in Washington, Secretary Ickes arranged for her to perform from the steps of

---

[16] Felix Frankfurter, "The Young Men Go to Washington," *Fortune*, XIII (1936), 61; E. W. Bakke, *Citizens Without Work* (New Haven: 1940), pp. 52–53.

[17] Richard Neuberger, "They Love Roosevelt," *Forum and Century*, CI (1939), 15; Corwin, *The President*, p. 471; William O. Douglas, *Being an American* (New York: 1948), p. 88.

Lincoln Memorial. Equal representation for religious groups became so well accepted that, as one priest wryly complained, one never saw a picture of a priest in a newspaper unless he was flanked on either side by a minister and a rabbi.

The devotion Roosevelt aroused owed much to the fact that the New Deal assumed the responsibility for guaranteeing every American a minimum standard of subsistence. Its relief programs represented an advance over the barbaric predepression practices that constituted a difference not in degree but in kind. One analyst wrote: "During the ten years between 1929 and 1939 more progress was made in public welfare and relief than in the three hundred years after this country was first settled." The Roosevelt administration gave such assistance not as a matter of charity but of right. This system of social rights was written into the Social Security Act. Other New Deal legislation abolished child labor in interstate commerce and, by putting a floor under wages and a ceiling on hours, all but wiped out the sweatshop.[18]

Roosevelt and his aides fashioned a government which consciously sought to make the industrial system more humane and to protect workers and their families from exploitation. In his acceptance speech in June, 1936, the President stated: "Governments can err, Presidents do make mistakes, but the immortal Dante tells us that divine justice weighs the sins of the cold-blooded and the sins of the warm-hearted in different scales.

"Better the occasional faults of a Government that lives in a spirit of charity than the constant omission of a Government frozen in the ice of its own indifference." Nearly everyone in the Roosevelt government was caught up to some degree by a sense of participation in something larger than themselves. A few days after he took office, one of the more conservative New Deal administrators wrote in his diary: "This should be a Gov't of humanity."[19]

---

[18] Josephine Chapin Brown, *Public Relief 1929–1939* (New York: 1940), p. ix; Thomas Paul Jenkin, *Reactions of Major Groups to Positive Government in the United States, 1930–1940* (University of California Publications in Political Science [Berkeley and Los Angeles: 1945]), p. 284.

[19] *Public Papers*, V, 235; J. F. T. O'Connor MS. Diary, June 25, 1933.

Chapter Three

Opposition to the New Deal

Opposition to the New Deal program began with the very first hint that the election of Franklin D. Roosevelt might bring about significant change in the political life of the nation. President Herbert C. Hoover clearly recognized the vast differences between himself and his eventual successor. In many ways, his speech, "The Consequences of the Proposed New Deal," was the forerunner of the entire attack made by conservative Republicans upon the New Deal during the 1930's. To Hoover, the proposed New Deal would not only hold back the economic recovery which he felt was close at hand, but would also radically alter the political structure of the nation. From the beginning of the Depression in 1929, Hoover was of the conviction that its causes were external and that the economy would eventually right itself in keeping with the inevitable laws of economics. He felt that the New Deal would seriously hinder the natural operation of forces making for recovery.

The Republican Party

Early Republican opposition was limited to the conservative wing of the party. Progressive Republican Senators such as Hiram Johnson of California, George Norris of Nebraska, William E. Borah of Idaho, and Robert La Follette of Wisconsin, had bolted the party to endorse Roosevelt during the election of 1932 and continued to support his policies in Congress.

In addition to organization rifts which rendered Republican opposition to the New Deal ineffectual, the party suffered from a misunderstanding of the changing nature of American society. The socioeconomic deprivation of millions of immigrants and minority groups who were caught in the throes of the Depression, and the need for a central agency to cope with the problems arising from a complex urban-industrial society, were clearly beyond the comprehension of many of the older Republicans.

The nature of the Republican opposition to the New Deal legislative program during the 1930's was generally suggestive of the party's difficulty in meeting the challenges of adjustment to modern industrialism. To the conservative Republicans in and out of Congress the New Deal represented a violation of the familiar relationship between government and the men who held the greatest economic power. The New Deal, which had its roots in the Populist–Progressive revolts, clearly posed a serious threat to their old order.

Correspondingly, the charges against Roosevelt and his program were frequently couched in emotional terms. Republican Senators and Representatives often referred to Roosevelt as a "dictator," a Hitler, Stalin, or Caligula; they argued against "big" government and called for a broader measure of states rights; they demanded regulation rather than "control" of big business, lamented the "over-centralization" of American society, railed against rising government debt, protested the many welfare measures and called for more reliance on individual initiative and the restoration of the "free enterprise" system. These arguments were often phrased in terms that had been used many times over but which still held meaning for millions of Americans; self-reliance, self-respect, laissez-faire, the universal laws of economics, frugality, states rights, personal freedom, presidential self-restraint, and the doubtful morality of an unbalanced budget.

The Republican attempt to right the alleged imbalance wrought by the New Deal revealed a basic weakness in their arguments. It was one thing to speak theoretically of returning the responsibilities and duties of relief, welfare, and unemployment to the state and local governments. It was still another to reconcile theory with the reality of economic distress. With approximately fifteen million persons unemployed, civic unrest, bank panics, and other serious problems, state and local agencies were ill-equipped to meet the needs of the day. Nor was it possible for the voluntary agencies, limited in their scope, to assume responsibility for the welfare programs.

Unable or unwilling to comprehend the changes which had occurred in American society — as aggravated and revealed in the Crash and Depression — Republicans suffered at the polls. With each succeeding congressional and presidential election in the 1930's, the Republican vote dwindled. The election of 1936 very nearly made the party into a memory. Republican candidate Alfred Landon of Kansas won just two states (Maine and Vermont) and polled about ten million popular votes less than Roosevelt. Of the 435 Representatives in the lower house, only eighty-eight were Republicans. In the Senate body of ninety-six, the party was even more heavily decimated; only about fifteen Republicans clustered in a small corner of the upper legislative house.

The cohesion and strength of the Republicans, however, began to improve in the years that followed and in the presidential election of 1940 they were again a relatively thriving party, though still in the minority. Nevertheless, despite the increase, the Republican Party was still bankrupt of programs and ideas. This state of affairs is revealed in the reprinted excerpt from a speech by Thomas E. Dewey, then Governor of New York and regarded as a liberal in the party. The fact that Dewey could do little more than point out how well the country had fared in the 1920's under Republican administrations was indicative of the paucity of Republican creativity. Consequently, in many vital issues, the effective opposition to the New Deal devolved to other groups in society.

The Non-Republican Opposition

The severity of the depression, the scope of the New Deal program, and the ineffectiveness of the Republican Party contributed to the development of a variety of other groups which criticized New Deal policies. Some of these criticisms embodied alternatives to the methods of the New Deal; others, however, were in direct opposition to the aims of the legislative enactments of the Democrats.

In the first category, for example, were the Townsend Clubs. Dr. Francis E. Townsend of Long Beach, California, was a former health officer living in dire economic circumstances. He was primarily concerned with the plight of the aged in society. Townsend proposed a monthly pension of two hundred dollars to all persons over the age of sixty provided that they would spend the money within thirty days. The extent of the economic difficulties of the elderly could be seen in the swift popular acceptance of his program: by 1935 there were over a thousand Townsend Clubs in rural and small-town areas across the country. Townsend's movement, however, was undercut by the passage of the Social Security Act in 1935.

Another powerful figure opposing Roosevelt was Father Charles E. Coughlin of Royal Oak, Michigan, one of the most colorful of radio personalities of the 1930's. Coughlin was an early supporter of the New Deal but eventually turned against Roosevelt and associated him with the "godless capitalists." Coughlin's attitudes were a mixture of anti-Semitism and quasi-socialistic schemes. As part of the program of his National Union for Social Justice, he called for currency inflation, a minimum annual wage, and the nationalization of banking and natural resources. Coughlin incurred the displeasure of the hierarchy of the Catholic Church for his anti-Semitic remarks and was forced to relinquish his radio program.

Of all the individuals who opposed the New Deal, none was more powerful and colorful than Huey Long, the "Kingfish" of Louisiana. At the time of his death by assassination in 1935, Long had established himself as the virtual dictator of Louisiana, having served as both Governor and Senator. His plan was called "Share the Wealth" (see the speech later in this chapter). Long argued that "every man ought to be a king" and began to build up a national following in the first two years of the New Deal. His influence was so great that Jim Farley, the Postmaster General and National Chairman of the Democratic Party, had estimates in 1935 which showed that if Long were to run for president on a third-party ticket in 1936 he might poll three million votes. Long, however, never had the opportunity to test Farley's assessment.

The Socialist Party, led by Norman Thomas, opposed the New Deal on the grounds that it was merely shoring up the essentially doomed capitalistic system. In the excerpt in this chapter, Thomas, one of the most respected Socialists of the twentieth century, dismisses the idea that the New Deal was socialistic and asks the question, After the New Deal, What?

The Communist Party of the United States was also unhappy with the New Deal but showed less consistency in its opposition. Basically, Communists felt that Roosevelt was a capitalist who was preventing the real revolution by throwing scraps to the proletariat in the form of unemployment relief, work programs, and the like. The opposition of the Communist Party vacillated in the late thirties when the Popular Front to fight against the fascist nations in Europe was organized.

On the other side of the political spectrum was the American Liberty League. Organized in 1934 by members of the upper economic brackets — dissident wealthy Democrats and outraged Republicans — the Liberty League attempted to pose as a nonpartisan group bent on assessing the merits of the New Deal. But its real purposes were quickly revealed in its emotionally-charged polemical publications. One of their pamphlets attacking the New Deal as being fascist and mercantilist — that is, anti-capitalistic — is reproduced in this section. The reader should take particular note of the comparison of the stance of the Liberty League and the Socialist Party — political voices at the opposite ends of the political spectrum.

Thus the New Deal engendered considerable opposition, which in many ways has continued into the contemporary period. What happened to these individuals and groups from outside the major parties? Essentially, they were all rendered ineffective after the election of 1936. In one of the most powerful electoral victories in American political history, Roosevelt swept the field of independent political radicalism. The right wing forces, organized into the Union Party, received 882,000 votes. Norman Thomas' Socialist Party vote had dwindled from 881,000 in 1932 to 187,000 in 1936. Earl Browder of the Communist Party made a bare showing in the final tally with 80,000 votes; four years before, William Z. Foster had received 102,000 votes. The Republican Party fared little better. In sum, the election of 1936 left the political scene with no strong groups to contest the New Deal.

But a year later, the New Deal was in serious trouble. A coalition of conservative Democrats (many, Southerners), and Republicans formed to fight the legislative program in Congress. The combining of forces would play havoc with New Deal legislation for the next twenty years. Before it could really rout the New Deal, however, the war intervened. It was not until the 80th Congress from 1946 to 1948 that the anti–New Deal forces were able to organize concerted resistance to the tide of political and economic changes.

The Consequences of the Proposed New Deal (1932)*

Herbert Hoover

This speech was delivered by Hoover in Madison Square Garden, New York, on October 31, 1932. The original address appears in full in *Campaign Speeches of 1932* (New York: Doubleday, Doran & Co., 1933). We are publishing extracts from an abridged version found in Hoover's *Addresses upon the American Road.*

This campaign is more than a contest between two men. It is more than a contest between two parties. It is a contest between two philosophies of government.

We are told by the opposition that we must have a change, that we must have a new deal. It is not the change that comes from normal development of national life to which I object, but the proposal to alter the whole foundations of our national life which have been builded through generations of testing and struggle, and of the principles upon which we have builded the nation. The expressions our opponents use must refer to important changes in our economic and social system and our system of government, otherwise they are nothing but vacuous words. And I realize that in this time of distress many of our people are asking whether our social and economic system is incapable of that great primary function of providing security and comfort of life to all of the firesides of our 25 million homes in America, whether our social system provides for the fundamental development and progress of our people, whether our form of government is capable of originating and sustaining that security and progress.

This question is the basis upon which our opponents are appealing to the people in their fears and distress. They are proposing changes and so-called new deals which would destroy the very foundations of our American system.

Our people should consider the primary facts before they come to the judgment—not merely through political agitation, the glitter of promise, and the discouragement of temporary hardships—whether they will support changes which radically affect the whole system which has been builded up by a hundred and fifty years of the toil of our fathers. They should not approach the question in the despair with which our opponents would clothe it.

---

* Reprinted with the permission of Charles Scribner's Sons from pages 1–3, 3–7, 15–16, 16–19 of *Addresses upon the American Road* by Herbert Hoover. Copyright 1938 Edgar Rickard; renewal copyright © 1966 Herbert Hoover, Jr.

Our economic system has received abnormal shocks during the last three years, which temporarily dislocated its normal functioning. These shocks have in a large sense come from without our borders, but I say to you that our system of government has enabled us to take such strong action as to prevent the disaster which would otherwise have come to our nation. It has enabled us further to develop measures and programs which are now demonstrating their ability to bring about restoration and progress.

We must go deeper than platitudes and emotional appeals of the public platform in the campaign, if we will penetrate to the full significance of the changes which our opponents are attempting to float upon the wave of distress and discontent from the difficulties we are passing through. We can find what our opponents would do after searching the record of their appeals to discontent, group and sectional interest. We must search for them in the legislative acts which they sponsored and passed in the Democratic-controlled House of Representatives in the last session of Congress. We must look into measures for which they voted and which were defeated. We must inquire whether or not the presidential and vice-presidential candidates have disavowed these acts. If they have not, we must conclude that they form a portion and are a substantial indication of the profound changes proposed.

And we must look still further than this as to what revolutionary changes have been proposed by the candidates themselves.

.   .   .   .

I may say at once that the changes proposed from all these Democratic principals and allies are of the most profound and penetrating character. If they are brought about this will not be the America which we have known in the past.

Let us pause for a moment and examine the American system of government, of social and economic life, which it is now proposed that we should alter. Our system is the product of our race and of our experience in building a nation to heights unparalleled in the whole history of the world. It is a system peculiar to the American people. It differs essentially from all others in the world. It is an American system.

It is founded on the conception that only through ordered liberty, through freedom to the individual, and equal opportunity to the individual, will his initiative and enterprise be summoned to spur the march of progress.

It is by the maintenance of equality of opportunity and therefore of a society absolutely fluid in freedom of the movement of its human particles that our individualism departs from the individualism of Europe.

We resent class distinction because there can be no rise for the individual through the frozen strata of classes and no stratification of classes can take place in a mass livened by the free rise of its particles. Thus in our ideals the able and ambitious are able to rise constantly from the bottom to leadership in the community.

This freedom of the individual creates of itself the necessity and the cheerful willingness of men to act cooperatively in a thousand ways and for every purpose as occasion arises; and it permits such voluntary cooperations to be dissolved as soon as they have served their purpose, to be replaced by new voluntary associations for new purposes.

There has thus grown within us, to gigantic importance, a new conception. That is, this voluntary cooperation within the community. Cooperation to perfect the social organizations; cooperation for the care of those in distress; cooperation for the advancement of knowledge, of scientific research, of education; for cooperative action in the advancement of many phases of economic life. This is self-government by the people outside of government; it is the most powerful development of individual freedom and equal opportunity that has taken place in the century and a half since our fundamental institutions were founded.

It is in the further development of this cooperation and a sense of its responsibility that we should find solution for many of our complex problems, and not by the extension of government into our economic and social life. The greatest function of government is to build up that cooperation, and its most resolute action should be to deny the extension of bureaucracy. We have developed great agencies of cooperation by the assistance of the government which promote and protect the interests of individuals and the smaller units of business. The Federal Reserve System, in its strengthening and support of the smaller banks; the Farm Board, in its strenghtening and support of the farm cooperatives; the Home Loan banks, in the mobilizing of building and loan associations and savings banks; the federal land banks, in giving independence and strength to land mortgage associations; the great mobilization of relief to distress, the mobilization of business and industry in measures of recovery, and a score of other activities are not socialism—they are the essence of protection to the development of free men.

The primary conception of this whole American system is not the regimentation of men but the cooperation of free men. It is founded upon the conception of responsibility of the individual to the community, of the responsibility of local government to the state, of the state to the national government.

It is founded on a peculiar conception of self-government designed to maintain this equal opportunity to the individual, and through decentralization it brings about and maintains these responsibilities. The centralization of government will undermine responsibilities and will destroy the system.

Our government differs from all previous conceptions, not only in this decentralization, but also in the separation of functions between the legislative, executive, and judicial arms of government, in which the independence of the judicial arm is the keystone of the whole structure.

It is founded on a conception that in times of emergency, when forces are running beyond control of individuals or other cooperative action, beyond the control of local communities and of states, then the great reserve powers of the federal government shall be brought into action to protect the community. But when these forces have ceased there must be a return of state, local, and individual responsibility.

The implacable march of scientific discovery with its train of new inventions presents every year new problems to government and new problems to the social order. Questions often arise whether, in the face of the growth of these new and gigantic tools, democracy can remain master in its own house, can preserve the fundamentals of our American system. I contend that it can; and I contend that this American system of ours has demonstrated its validity and superiority over any system yet invented by the human mind.

It has demonstrated it in the face of the greatest test of our history— that is the emergency which we have faced in the last three years.

When the political and economic weakness of many nations of Europe, the result of the World War and its aftermath, finally culminated in collapse of their institutions, the delicate adjustments of our economic and social life received a shock unparalleled in our history. No one knows that better than you of New York. No one knows its causes better than you. That the crisis was so great that many of the leading banks sought directly or indirectly to convert their assets into gold or its equivalent with the result that they practically ceased to function as credit institutions; that many of our citizens sought flight for their capital to other countries; that many of them attempted to hoard gold in large amounts. These were but indications of the flight of confidence and of the belief that our government could not overcome these forces.

Yet these forces were overcome—perhaps by narrow margins—and this action demonstrates what the courage of a nation can accomplish under the resolute leadership in the Republican Party. And I say the Republican Party because our opponents, before and during the crises, proposed no constructive program; though some of their members patriotically supported ours. Later on the Democratic House of Representatives did develop the real thought and ideas of the Democratic Party, but it was so destructive that it had to be defeated, for it would have destroyed, not healed.

In spite of all these obstructions we did succeed. Our form of government did prove itself equal to the task. We saved this nation from a quarter of a century of chaos and degeneration, and we preserved the savings, the insurance policies, gave a fighting chance to men to hold their homes. We saved the integrity of our government and the honesty of the American dollar. And we installed measures which today are bringing back recovery. Employment, agriculture, business—all of these show the steady, if slow, healing of our enormous wound.

I therefore contend that the problem of today is to continue these measures and policies to retore this American system to its normal functioning, to repair the wounds it has received, to correct the weaknesses and evils which would defeat that system. To enter upon a series of deep changes to embark upon this inchoate new deal which has been propounded in this campaign would be to undermine and destroy our American system.

.   .   .   .

If these measures, these promises, which I have discussed; or these failures to disavow these projects; this attitude of mind, mean anything, they mean the enormous expansion of the federal government; they mean the growth of bureaucracy such as we have never seen in our history. No man who has not occupied my position in Washington can fully realize the constant battle which must be carried on against incompetence, corruption, tyranny of government expanded into business activities. If we first examine the effect on our form of government of such a program, we come at once to the effect of the most gigantic increase in expenditure ever known in history. That alone would break down the savings, the wages, the equality of opportunity among our people. These measures would transfer vast responsibilities to the federal government from the states, the local governments, and the individuals. But that is not all; they would break down our form of government. Our legislative bodies cannot delegate their authority to any dictator, but without such delegation every member of these bodies is impelled in representation of the interest of his constituents constantly to seek privilege and demand service in the use of such agencies. Every time the federal government extends its arm, 531 Senators and Congressmen become actual boards of directors of that business.

.   .   .   .

We have heard a great deal in this campaign about reactionaries, conservatives, progressives, liberals, and radicals. I have not yet heard an attempt by any one of the orators who mouth these phrases to define the principles upon which they base these classifications. There is one thing I can say without any question of doubt—that is, that the spirit of liberalism is to create free men; it is not the regimentation of men. It is not the extension of bureaucracy. I have said in this city before now that you cannot extend the mastery of government over the daily life of a people without somewhere making it master of people's souls and thoughts. Expansion of government in business means that the government, in order to protect itself from the political consequences of its errors, is driven irresistibly without peace to greater and greater control of the nation's press and platform. Free speech does not live many hours after free industry and free commerce die. It is a false liberalism that interprets itself into government operation of business. Every step in that direction poisons the very roots of liberalism. It poisons political equality, free speech, free press, and equality of opportunity. It is the road not to liberty but to less liberty. True liberalism is found not in striving to spread bureaucracy, but in striving to set bounds to it. True liberalism seeks all legitimate freedom first in the confident belief that without such freedom the pursuit of other blessings is in vain. Liberalism is a force truly of the spirit proceeding from the deep realization that economic freedom cannot be sacrificed if political freedom is to be preserved.

Even if the government conduct of business could give us the maximum of efficiency instead of least efficiency, it would be purchased at the cost of freedom. It would increase rather than decrease abuse and corruption, stifle initiative and invention, undermine development of leadership, cripple mental and spiritual energies of our people, extinguish equality of opportunity, and dry up the spirit of liberty and progress. Men who are going about this country announcing that they are liberals because of their promises to extend the government in business are not liberals, they are reactionaries of the United States.

And I do not wish to be misquoted or misunderstood. I do not mean that our government is to part with one iota of its national resources without complete protection to the public interest. I have already stated that democracy must remain master in its own house. I have stated that abuse and wrongdoing must be punished and controlled. Nor do I wish to be misinterpreted as stating that the United States is a free-for-all and devil-take-the-hindermost society.

The very essence of equality of opportunity of our American system is that there shall be no monopoly or domination by any group or section in this country, whether it be business, sectional, or a group interest. On the contrary, our American system demands economic justice as well as political and social justice; it is not a system of laissez faire.

I am not setting up the contention that our American system is perfect. No human ideal has ever been perfectly attained, since humanity itself is not perfect. But the wisdom of our forefathers and the wisdom of the thirty men who have preceded me in this office hold to the conception that progress can be attained only as the sum of accomplishments of free individuals, and they have held unalterably to these principles.

In the ebb and flow of economic life our people in times of prosperity and ease naturally tend to neglect the vigilance over their rights. Moreover, wrongdoing is obscured by apparent success in enterprise. Then insidious diseases and wrongdoings grow apace. But we have in the past seen in times of distress and difficulty that wrongdoing and weakness come to the surface, and our people, in their endeavors to correct these wrongs, are tempted to extremes which may destroy rather than build.

It is men who do wrong, not our institutions. It is men who violate the laws and public rights. It is men, not institutions, who must be punished.

In my acceptance speech four years ago at Palo Alto I stated that—

> One of the oldest aspirations of the human race was the abolition of poverty. By poverty I mean the grinding by under-nourishment, cold, ignorance, fear of old age to those who have the will to work.

I stated that—

> In America today we are nearer a final triumph over poverty than in any land. The poorhouse has vanished from among us; we have not reached that goal, but given a chance to go forward, we shall, with the help of God, be in sight of the day when poverty will be banished from this nation.

.   .   .   .

My countrymen, the proposals of our opponents represent a profound change in American life—less in concrete proposal, bad as that may be, than by implication and by evasion. Dominantly in their spirit they represent a radical departure from the foundations of 150 years which have made this the greatest nation in the world. This election is not a mere shift from the ins to the outs. It means deciding the direction our nation will take over a century to come.

The Seven Lean Years (1940)*

Thomas E. Dewey

This is an excerpt, as published later by Dewey, of a speech made at Louisville, Kentucky on May 11, 1940.

For seven years now our government in Washington has been controlled by prophets of despair. For seven years the Administration has fumbled with unemployment and economic want.

And after seven years of fumbling, what are the results?—ten and a half million men still unemployed. And what is the New Deal answer to the problem of unemployment? Its answer is surrender. The New Deal says: It cannot be solved.

That I am here to deny. I say to you: it can be solved. This country demands an administration that believes it can be solved.

We cannot always live huddled together, afraid to move, while those who control our destiny tell us there is no other course. America is not a nation of children, to be tied to the apron-strings of government. America is not 130 million people who have quit because they have reached a frontier.

Progress is not bounded by geography. The progress of a great people does not stop when its boundaries are reached. To a great nation there is no last frontier. Within our own land there are endless worlds to conquer. The only limits of progress are limits of energy and spirit.

Next November there is an election. Next November the New Deal expects the American people to march to the polls and vote "yes." But the American people remember what happened after 1936. There will be no "mandate" for the New Dealers this November.

I want to discuss with you briefly some of the evidence bearing on the issues before us.

First, on the economic side. Let us consider the New Deal record. Let us take its seven years and compare them with the preceding seven years—Republican years.

Compare the averages of the seven Republican years with the averages of the seven New Deal years. That gives the New Deal a great advantage, since the Republican period included three years of world depression. But let them have that advantage. They need it.

---

* From pp. 52–56, "The Seven Lean Years," from *The Case Against the New Deal* by Thomas E. Dewey. Copyright 1940 by Harper & Brothers. Reprinted by permission of Harper & Row, Publishers.

Here are the results of the comparison. First among the items is national income.

National Income: Down. From $70 billion average in the Republican years to $62 billion in the New Deal years.

The next item is farm income.

Farm Income: (Including all government payments) *Down.* From $9 billion in the Republican years to $7.5 billion in the New Deal years.

And then some more:

Agricultural Exports: Down. From $1.5 billion to less than three-quarters of a billion dollars a year.

Farm Prices: Down. Nearly 20 per cent.

Industrial Wages and Salaries: Down. From $21 billion to $16.5 billion.

Dividend Payments: Down. From $4.5 billion to $3 billion.

New Capital Invested: Down. From $4 billion to less than one billion.

New Building: Down. More than 50 per cent.

There is not much of a campaign document for the New Deal in those figures.

But the New Deal suggests that the amount of income is not important. They say it is distribution of income that counts. But when the total income of every group is less, the hard fact is that the New Deal has only succeeded in redistributing poverty. The only important redistribution of income under the New Deal has been out of the pockets of the American people and into the hands of the Washington bureaucrats.

That redistribution has been immense.

And that brings us to another set of items in our comparison—the "up" items. Oh yes, there have been increases under the New Deal. Not everything has gone down. Some averages, and very important ones, have gone up between the seven Republican years and the seven New Deal years.

Here are some items from that list.

Employees on the Federal Payroll: Up. From an average of 550,000 in the Republican years to 770,000 in the New Deal years. And it's nearly a million now.

Taxes: Up. From three and a third billion dollars per year for the Republican average to nearly $5 billion for the New Deal average. And they're $5.5 billion now.

Expenditures of Government: Up. From $3.5 billion a year to over $8 billion under the New Deal. And they're over $9 billion now.

Annual Government Deficit: Up. From one-fifth of a billion dollars per year average to $3.5 billion under the New Deal. And this year it will be $4 billion.

And finally, *Industrial Disputes: Up.* From 800 to 2500 a year.

There is the picture—the seven lean years. National income down, farm income down, farm prices down, farm exports down, labor income down, dividends down, new building down, the flow of private investment—the stream that turns the wheels of business—reduced to a trickle.

And on the other hand, unemployment up—up to over 10 million, while the bureaucratic establishment has doubled. Annual deficit astronomical. And the National Debt more than doubled since 1933.

There are the ups and the downs. Things that should be down are up. Things that should be up are down. The measures of incompetence up, the measures of prosperity down.

There in two short lists is the indictment for economic failure. There is the record on which the New Deal has to stand. There is the record on which the New Deal will fall.

Every Man a King (1934)*

Senator Huey Long

Is that a right of life, when the young children of this country are being reared into a sphere which is more owned by twelve men than it is by 120 million people?

.   .   .   .

It is not the difficulty of the problem which we have; it is the fact that the rich people of this country—and by rich people I mean the super-rich—will not allow us to solve the problems, or rather the one little problem that is afflicting this country, because in order to cure all of our woes it is necessary to scale down the big fortunes, that we may scatter the wealth to be shared by all of the people.

We have a marvelous love for this government of ours; in fact, it is almost a religion, and it is well that it should be, because we have a splendid form of government and we have a splendid set of laws. We have everything here that we need, except that we have neglected the fundamentals upon which the American government was principally predicated.

---

* Excerpts from a radio speech given over the National Broadcasting System on February 23, 1934 by the Senator from Louisiana. Taken from the *Congressional Record* (March 1, 1934), 3450–52.

How many of you remember the first thing that the Declaration of Independence said? It said, "We hold these truths to be self-evident, that there are certain inalienable rights for the people, and among them are life, liberty, and the pursuit of happiness"; and it said, further, "We hold the view that all men are created equal."

Now, what did they mean by that? Did they mean, my friends, to say that all men were created equal and that meant that any one man was born to inherit $10 million and that another child was to be born to inherit nothing?

Did that mean, my friends, that someone would come into this world without having had an opportunity, of course, to have hit one lick of work, should be born with more than it and all of its children and children's children could ever dispose of, but that another one would have to be born into a life of starvation?

That was not the meaning of the Declaration of Independence when it said that all men are created equal or "That we hold that all men are created equal."

Nor was it the meaning of the Declaration of Independence when it said that they held that there were certain rights that were inalienable—the right of life, liberty, and the pursuit of happiness.

Is that a right of life, my friends, when the young children of this country are being reared into a sphere which is more owned by twelve men than it is by 120 million people?

Is that, my friends, giving them a fair shake of the dice or anything like the inalienable right of life, liberty, and the pursuit of happiness, or anything resembling the fact that all people are created equal; when we have today in America thousands and hundreds of thousands and millions of children on the verge of starvation in a land that is overflowing with too much to eat and too much to wear?

.   .   .   .

Now, we have organized a society, and we call it "Share Our Wealth Society," a society with the motto "every man a king."

Every man a king, so there would be no such thing as a man or woman who did not have the necessities of life, who would not be dependent upon the whims and caprices and ipse dixit of the financial martyrs [masters?] for a living. What do we propose by this society? We propose to limit the wealth of big men in the country. There is an average of $15,000 in wealth to every family in America. That is right here today.

We do not propose to divide it up equally. We do not propose a division of wealth, but we propose to limit poverty that we will allow to be inflicted upon any man's family. We will not say we are going to try to guarantee any equality, or $15,000 to families. No; but we do say that one-third of the average is low enough for any one family to hold, that there should be a guaranty of a family wealth of around $5,000; enough for a home, an automobile, a radio, and the ordinary conveniences, and the opportunity to educate their children; a fair share of the income of this land thereafter to that family so there will be no such thing as merely the select to have those things, and so there will be no such thing as a family living in poverty and distress.

We have to limit fortunes. Our present plan is that we will allow no one man to own more than $50 million. We think that with that limit we will be able to carry out the balance of the program. It may be necessary that we limit it to less than $50 million. It may be necessary, in working out of the plans, that no man's fortune would be more than $10 million or $15 million. But be that as it may, it will still be more than any one man, or any one man and his children and their children, will be able to spend in their lifetimes; and it is not necessary or reasonable to have wealth piled up beyond that point where we cannot prevent poverty among the masses.

Another thing we propose is old-age pension of $30 a month for everyone that is sixty years old. Now, we do not give this pension to a man making $1,000 a year, and we do not give it to him if he has $10,000 in property, but outside of that we do.

We will limit hours of work. There is not any necessity of having overproduction. I think all you have got to do, ladies and gentlemen, is just limit the hours of work to such an extent as people will work only so long as is necessary to produce enough for all of the people to have what they need. Why, ladies and gentlemen, let us say that all of these labor-saving devices reduce hours down to where you do not have to work but four hours a day; that is enough for these people, and then praise be the name of the Lord, if it gets that good. Let it be good and not a curse, and then we will have five hours a day and five days a week, or even less than that, and we might give a man a whole month off during a year, or give him two months; and we might do what other countries have seen fit to do, and what I did in Louisiana, by having schools by which adults could go back and learn the things that have been discovered since they went to school.

We will not have any trouble taking care of the agricultural situation. All you have to do is balance your production with your consumption. You simply have to abandon a particular crop that you have too much of, and all you have to do is store the surplus for the next year, and the government will take it over. When you have good crops in the area in which the crops that have been planted are sufficient for another year, put in your public works in the particular year when you do not need to raise any more, and by that means you get everybody employed. When the government has enough of any particular crop to take care of all of the people, that will be all that is necessary; and in order to do all of this, our taxation is going to be to take the billion-dollar fortunes and strip them down to frying size, not to exceed $50 million, and if it is necessary to come to $10 million, we will come to $10 million. We have worked the proposition out to guarantee a limit upon property (and no man will own less than one-third the average), and guarantee a reduction of fortunes and a reduction of hours to spread wealth throughout this country. We would care for the old people above sixty and take them away from this thriving industry, and give them a chance to enjoy the necessities and live in ease, and thereby lift from the market the labor which would probably create a surplus of commodities.

Those are the things we propose to do. "Every man a king." Every man to eat when there is something to eat; all to wear something when there is something to wear. That makes us all a sovereign.

.   .   .   .

Get together in your community tonight or tomorrow and organize one of our Share Our Wealth societies. If you do not understand it, write me and let me send you the platform; let me give you the proof of it.

This is Huey P. Long talking, United States Senator, Washington, D.C. Write me and let me send you the data on this proposition. Enroll with us. Let us make known to the people what we are going to do. I will send you a button, if I have got enough of them left. We have got a little button that some of our friends designed, with our message around the rim of the button, and in the center "Every man a king." Many thousands of them are meeting through the United States, and every day we are getting hundreds and hundreds of letters. Share Our Welath societies are now being organized, and people have it within their power to relieve themselves from this terrible situation.

What Was the New Deal? (1936)*

Norman Thomas

It is a testimony to the economic illiteracy of America that the New Deal has been called almost everything from communism and socialism

* Chapter II, "What Was the New Deal?" in Norman Thomas, *After the New Deal, What?* (New York: The Macmillan Co., 1936), pp. 16–21. Reprinted with the permission of The Macmillan Company from *After the New Deal, What?* by Norman Thomas. Copyright 1936 by Norman Thomas, renewed 1964 by Norman Thomas.

to fascism. Or, as one editor put it: "Socialism or Fascism—What's the difference? We don't like it." Actually the New Deal is, or rather was, an experimental attempt at reformed capitalism. Part of the time Mr. Roosevelt talked, and practiced very little, the gospel of the virtue of smallness. Little business was, he has said or implied, pretty good. His effort to break up big utility holding companies looked in that direction. He made gestures toward it in some of his tax proposals. His declaration of a war of liberation against "economic dynasties" in his acceptance speech can be interpreted as a modern renewal of the struggle of the in-dividual against the growth of concentration of control in the hands of the masters of finance capital. But his main reliance has been state cap-italism; that is a degree of government ownership and a much greater degree of government regulation of economic enterprises for the sake of bolstering up the profit system.

It was not socialism. The argument to the contrary was born partly from the American delusion that government ownership equals socialism and government regulation approaches it. That depends, of course, on who owns the government, and for what purpose the government owns industry: for war and militarism; for greater security of banking as a better instrument of the profit system, or for the sake of planned abun-dance for all.

There is, however, more definite reason why "Mr. John Q. Public" should think the New Deal and Mr. Roosevelt's present efforts are social-istic. He has been told so in various accounts by Mr. David Lawrence, Mr. Alfred Emanuel Smith and Mr. James P. Warburg, whose book *Hell Bent for Election* has been circulated as a campaign document. In Denver one of my Socialist friends was assured by a woman that it was entirely unnecessary for her to hear Mr. Thomas talk about socialism. She knew all about it. Mr. Warburg's book had told her that the New Deal was socialism and she knew all about the New Deal!

Now as everybody knows, or ought to know, the essence of socialism lies in the end of the class division of income; that is, in planned produc-tion for the general use rather than for the private profit of an owning class. Such planned production requires the social ownership of the great natural resources and the principal means of production and distribu-tion. To this principle Mr. Roosevelt has not even professed allegiance; rather he has declared his support of a profit system that in one of his official addresses he inaccurately defined. Only in the Tennessee Valley Authority is there an approximation of a socialist approach to a great economic problem. For the rest Mr. Roosevelt put the banks in order and turned them back to the bankers; he set an able administrator or co-ordinator, Mr. Joseph B. Eastman, over the railroads, not to socialize them but to help to pull them out of depression primarily for the benefit of private stockholders whose railway holdings will thereby be made more expensive if and when the government takes them over.

That such a program should be confused with socialism by special pleaders like Mr. Warburg is perhaps in part the fault of European socialists who in office have so often been concerned only with reforms attainable within capitalism. It may be a little our fault in America that in our Socialist platform of 1932 we did not distinguish more plainly between immediate demands and our essential revolutionary purpose. But only a little. The Socialist platform of 1932 in its opening paragraphs gives the Socialist diagnosis of poverty and insecurity. It declares for socialization in more than one section. Mr. Warburg makes a plausible case that Mr. Roosevelt has carried out the Socialist platform by a highly selective choice of Socialist demands, and by a very superficial test of what it would mean to carry out effectively even those demands to which Mr. Roosevelt apparently paid some heed.

For example, during years of boondoggling and other forms of made work, public housing in the sense in which we Socialists developed our demand for it in 1932 and 1933 was grossly neglected. Only toward the end of the four-year term did Senator [Robert] Wagner introduce his inadequate public housing bill which was not on the President's *must* list. Congress adjourned without passing it. The next Congress, even assuming Mr. Roosevelt's election, is likely to be less, not more, progressive in this matter. With a third of our people housed in shacks and slums fit only for destruction, the builders and the workers in materials were kept in unemployment on a miserable dole or some form of improvised or comparatively non-essential public work. And they call this socialism!

Or, to take an even more striking example: When the President finally got around to security legislation, long dear to the hearts of Socialists, he took the name rather than the substance of any Socialist proposal. Intelligent Socialists vigorously repudiate any responsibility for the President's so-called Security Bill. This omnibus measure neglects altogether the vital matter of health insurance or any equivalent for it. Its immediate allowance to the states for old age assistance is meager. The reserve to be set up for old age insurance is very large and the manner of its investment makes for a dangerous degree of political control over business in the future, without in the least changing the basic principles of that control from those appropriate to capitalism to those which would be necessary under a cooperative commonwealth.

Worst of all, however, is the treatment given to unemployment insurance. The federal government has set a certain tax on payrolls; ninety per cent of this tax to be rebated to employers who may come under state unemployment insurance schemes for the support of such schemes. Under the most favorable circumstances, the amount thus rebated cannot provide more than a fifteen-week period of insurance at a rate not to exceed $15 a week. The plan would work out somewhat as follows:

If you are now unemployed your chance of being helped by unemployment insurance depends upon your getting a job. You must hold a job while the reserve piles up in the Federal Treasury and while the state of which you are a citizen works out its own unemployment insurance plan. Then if you lose the job you may possibly get $15 a week for fifteen weeks provided the optimistic calculations of the amount to be received are correct, and provided your particular state takes advantage of the law and sets up its own machinery for insurance. There are forty-eight states. There will be forty-eight different systems—if all the states get around to providing unemployment insurance which is more than all of them have yet done in the case of workmen's compensation. There will be enormous confusion. The benefits to the unemployed will be kept down because of the fear of each state that adequate insurance measures will drive corporations into the borders of other states less generous in their treatment of the workers. The payroll tax itself will to a large extent be passed on to consumers; that is, the workers themselves, in an increase in prices. It will be added to the immense volume of indirect taxation or of sales taxes under which the American worker now struggles. Moreover the tax on employers as the sole support of unemployment insurance will inevitably spur them to reduce it by reducing the number of their employees. It will stimulate technological unemployment.

This is not socialism—not even what Mr. David Lawrence calls "unconscious socialism." The most that one can say is that in 1933 President Roosevelt had to act in a crisis. The principles to guide any effective action were not to be found in his own platform, and certainly not in the musty Republican document. Like many a politician before him, he had to turn to ideas advanced by Socialists. The trouble is not that he took some of them, but that he took so few and carried them out so unsatisfactorily. The moral of the tale is that if you want a child brought up right you better leave him with his parents, not turn him over to unsympathetic strangers.

Economic Planning — Mistaken but Not New (1935)*

Economic planning was no novelty to the framers of the Constitution. The people of the American colonies for more than a century had suffered from regulation of their trade by empire planners. The restrictions of those days, which were among the foremost causes of the Revolution, have their counterpart in present-day control of industry and agriculture by a federal bureaucracy. For years before the smoldering resentment finally broke into the flame of the Revolutionary War there had been a system of regulatory policies under the name of mercantilism. Today in the United States a similar system is called the New Deal. In European countries where private property is still recognized it is known as fascism.

King George II was the symbol of the autocratic power against which the colonies revolted. The twenty-seven grievances enumerated in the Declaration of Independence were directed specifically against him. Under New Deal laws and usurpations of authority, autocratic power to plan the course of economic affairs has become centered in the President of the United States who in his inaugural message on March 4, 1933, served notice that he would ask "broad executive power to wage a war against the emergency, as great as the power that would be given to me if we were in fact invaded by a foreign foe." In Italy Mussolini and in Germany Hitler typify autocracy and a planned economic order.

In making comparisons with existing governments there are points of similarity between the New Deal economic planning and Soviet Communism as well as fascism. Neither the New Deal nor fascism, however, abolishes private property and the capitalistic system as does Communism, although both encroach upon them. Under Communism, which purports to elevate the proletariat to a position of dominance but nevertheless operates under a dictatorship, there is a centralization in the state of authority over all economic activities just as in fascism and as attempted in the New Deal. In passing it may be noted that the economic planning of the present administration closely resembles in many regards the five-year plans of the Soviet government.

Some who now desire the Constitution changed to give free rein to the planning of all our daily affairs seek to convey the impression that regimentation had never been thought of in the "horse and buggy" days and that the framers of that historic document failed to anticipate the need of modern phases of regulation considered necessary by the "brain

---

* From a pamphlet by the same title issued as Document No. 75 by the American Liberty League (November, 1935), Washington, D.C., pp. 2–4, 5–6, 7–8, 13–15.

trust." The fact is that the colonists were the victims of economic planning, and the constitutional structure erected by the new nation was designed to furnish safeguards against economic experimentation conducted by a centralized authority. In the time that has intervened the Constitution has proved a strong and effective obstacle against complete control of the lives and activities of the people, just as its framers intended that it should. In the founding of our nation the states surrendered to the federal government authority over only such commerce as was of an interstate or foreign character, thus guarding against control by a centralized authority such as that to which the colonists had been subject.

What was the situation of the colonies prior to their war for independence?

Under economic planning as practiced by a centralized power in London, affecting not only the overseas trade of the colonies but their domestic activities as well, the welfare of the empire as viewed by the dominant British aristocrats was all that mattered. The planners held they were doing what was best for the empire as a whole, regardless of injuries or injustices inflicted upon individuals or groups. The colonists were not permitted to have anything to say about it.

The present Administration has planned similarly along lines held by its brain trust to be for the best interests of the nation as a whole. The people have had little voice in the program as carried out under general authority delegated unconstitutionally by the Congress to the President and his aides.

The Administration which put this program into effect was elected upon a specific platform. Not only did that platform contain no suggestion of regimentation for either industry or agriculture but, on the contrary, it voiced a striking denunciation of such a course. It promised the removal of government from fields of private enterprise and it condemned "the unsound policy of restricting agricultural products to the demands of domestic markets." This quotation is taken directly from the Democratic platform of 1932 which was endorsed by the presidential candidate 100 per cent.

The principle underlying the New Deal, like that governing the regulation of colonial trade before the revolution, was similar to the motivating influence of the policies of Fascist Italy. In fascism there is denial of the ability of the majority of the people to decide what is best for a nation. The welfare of the nation as determined by a dictator is the prime consideration; that of individuals of secondary importance. An autocratic power is held to be desirable. National Socialism in Germany embodies fascist principles.

.   .   .   .

Three Common Features

The New Deal, mercantilism and fascism have three chief characteristics in common, as follows:

1) All three contemplate a broad control of our working lives and activities along lines planned by the politicians in power. In the case of the New Deal this is shown in the attempt to expand the power of the federal government under the commerce clause of the Constitution and to use power under the revenue clause for purposes of regulation. New Deal policies do violence to our Constitution and our form of government while economic control is always a part of mercantilism and fascism.

2) In all three there is a governing class which considers itself an aristocracy of intelligence and morality. The executive branch of the government under the New Deal has usurped the functions of Congress in violation of the Constitution. Planning is in the hands of the President and his staff. In Italy parliamentary authority has been weakened almost to the point of destruction. The American colonies were regulated and taxed without the right of representation in the government.

3) Under dominant theories of all three the interests of individuals are subordinate to the welfare of the state. In the New Deal this characteristic is typified by policies which have been attacked in the courts on the ground of violation of the due process clause of the Constitution. Redistribution of wealth as proposed through New Deal tax legislation and other measures is based on the principle that those who have property must share it with others for the welfare of the entire nation. Under mercantilism working classes were forced to live on subsistence wages in order that English manufactured goods might be sold abroad at prices comparing favorably with those of other nations. In Italy workers are denied the right to strike because it is inimical to the welfare of the state. Private property is tolerated but is subject to confiscation. In all

three types of government, liberties of individuals are
sharply restricted under the pretense of benefiting the
state.

.   .   .   .

Beginnings of Planning

In the economic planning of the present day the system of rigid
control of industry and agriculture has been applied as part of a sudden
change in policies. Within less than a year after the Roosevelt Administration came into power a far-reaching system of control was in effect.
The systems of planned economies in Italy, Germany and Russia also
took shape rapidly.

.   .   .   .

There is nothing essentially new about economic planning. The planners under the New Deal have more governmental machinery through
which to carry out their program. They have more money to spend.
They have more elaborate blueprints and reports. But they are trying
to do the same thing that many earlier planners tried to do, namely, to
guide and control economic laws.

Mercantilism in the later Middle Ages represents only one of many
experiments in planning. In ancient China managed economies go back
to a very early date. The Chinese in the fifth century B.C. sought to
fix and maintain prices at substantially an unchanging level which was
presumed to represent equity for both the producer and the consumer.
China had a public works program in the building of the Great Wall.
The people of ancient Sparta were regimented. The Roman Empire was
a victim of planned economy. Its experiences with planning reached
their height under Diocletian who in the fourth century A.D. sought to
fix maximum prices for all sorts of commodities and services, with the
death penalty for violation. In the Byzantine Empire a few centuries
later prices were controlled through trade guilds and a redistribution of
wealth was attempted. Some germs of present-day planned economy
can be found in the feudalism and guilds of the Middle Ages.

The striking point with respect to economic planning wherever attempted is that it involves a different system of government than that
to which the United States has become accustomed under its Constitution. Economic planning may appear to succeed for a time under an
autocracy or dictatorship. It is out of place in a democracy. The liberties
and freedom of individual initiative which have marked the American

industrial system necessarily would be checked under a rigid governmental control of all economic activities.

The New Deal in its attempt to regiment and control industry and agriculture has departed from principles of government established under the Constitution. This departure from constitutional principles has taken definite lines as indicated by the three points of similarity with mercantilism and fascism already outlined. In adopting policies which are thus susceptible of comparison the New Deal has flouted the limitations upon economic control under the commerce clause of the Constitution, ignored the separation of powers in three coordinate branches of the government and ridden roughshod over the prohibitions in the Constitution against the taking of property without due process of law. The scores of cases now in the courts involving the commerce clause, delegation of power to the executive and the due process clause make it impossible to sustain denials by the New Deal of the charge that the maintenance of our form of government is at stake.

The people of the American colonies revolted against the rule of an autocratic government which sought to control economic activities. The framers of the Constitution were wise enough to devise an instrument under which it would be difficult again to exercise such far-reaching power. The limitations in the Constitution were intended to insure the maintenance of democratic principles. Through attempted control of economic activities under the New Deal these principles are being endangered.

Chapter Four

The Post-War Years: Continuing Opposition

The Second World War merely postponed the political struggle between the liberal proponents of the New Deal program and the opposition forces. By the close of the war, however, the economic and political picture had altered considerably. President Franklin D. Roosevelt had died suddenly just before the end of hostilities and in his place was the virtually unknown former senator from Missouri, Harry S. Truman. The new president had enormous problems to grapple with, not the least of which was a significant political change in the composition of Congress.

Campaigning on the slogan "Had Enough? Vote Republican," the Republicans were swept back into power in the Senate and House of Representatives in 1946 for the first time in almost two decades. The midterm election was disastrous for the Democrats on other levels as well; across the country New Dealers were turned out of state and local positions. Truman was thus confronted with a conservative atmosphere and a Republican Congress which he dubbed "That Good for Nothing Eightieth Congress" during the 1948 election campaign. Led by a coalition of Southern Democrats and conservative Republicans, the Eightieth Congress rejected Truman's domestic program. And both the Republicans and the dissident States Rights Democrats (headed by Governor Strom Thurmond of South Carolina) campaigned vigorously against Truman's re-labeled New Deal approach in the presidential campaign.

The essence of conservative arguments is summed up in the reprinted speech by Senator Robert A. Taft of Ohio. The son of President and Chief Justice of the Supreme Court, William Howard Taft, Robert Taft had become one of the most powerful Republicans in the Party and in Congress. As chairman of the Senate Republican Policy Committee, Taft utilized the anti–New Deal coalition to thwart Truman's programs and to push his own proposals of economy in government and controls over labor. Taft's Republicanism, however, was tempered by his support of such programs as low-cost housing, federal grants to states for education, and medical aid. The excerpt in this chapter is taken from Taft's reply to a speech made by President Truman in January, 1948.

The major complaint of the conservatives in the thirties had been that the federal government had no business competing with private enterprise — especially since the government operated on a deficit basis. There were bitter cries against the creation of the Tennessee Valley Authority, financial support for agricultural research, and government-sponsored projects in the performing arts. Such arguments have been repeated often. A speech of 1950 by Congressman Noah Mason of Illinois is included in this chapter as an indication of the conservative businessman's viewpoint. Mason was particularly unhappy about the growing public debt. While he did not call for the elimination of defense spending — which was responsible for much of the deficit — Mason did blame the necessity for large defense budgets on F.D.R.'s policy during World War II, especially in relation to the Soviet Union.

The anti–New Deal arguments of the left during the post-war period were similarly descended from the positions of the 1930's. In the Preamble to their 1948 party platform, the Socialists claimed that while the Democrats and Republicans "pretend they have solutions" to serious American problems, in reality they use tired cliches and offer outmoded programs. The Socialist platform detailed some specific suggestions for significant change, amounting to an outspoken demand for a restructured socialist society as a meaningful alternative to the half-hearted continuation of the New Deal program.

Also among the left opposition in the 1948 presidential elections was the new Progressive Party, led by Henry A. Wallace who had been first Secretary of Agriculture and then Vice President (1940–1944) under Roosevelt. Focusing mainly on international issues, the Progressives called for an end to the Cold War, which they felt could be accomplished through more sympathetic dealings with the Soviet Union. While some Socialists joined the Progressive Party, the majority avoided its ranks. But the Progressives gathered a substantial number of other left–radicals, including some members of the Communist Party.

With this much opposition to Truman from the left, the Republicans (and many other Americans) expected that Thomas Dewey would capture the presidency in the elections of 1948, and that the New Deal would be rejected *in toto* by the electorate. To their amazement, Truman defeated Dewey in that memorable election.

Thus, instead of turning back the New Deal, Republicans and conservatives found themselves confronting Truman's Fair Deal program. With the addition of heavy emphasis on civil rights, Truman's plan was essentially an extension of the original objectives of the New Deal. Frustrated by their defeat in 1948, the Republicans began to cast about for a candidate who might more successfully challenge the Democrats.

Dwight D. Eisenhower's name had been mentioned as a possible presidential nominee many times following his successful leadership of the Allied forces during World War II. One of the difficulties in considering his candidacy, however, was that nobody knew Eisenhower's party affiliation. So nonpartisan did he appear in his public and private statements that President Truman sounded out Eisenhower as the possible Democratic candidate for 1952. To the joy of most Republicans, however, Eisenhower declared himself to be oriented toward the Republican philosophy of government.

During his emergence as a political figure and then as a presidential candidate, Eisenhower voiced a brand of Republicanism akin to Senator Taft's. The tenor of his speeches during the campaign was firmly within the anti–New Deal tradition. Once elected, he felt that he had a mission to reconstruct the government along conservative lines, as indicated by the title of his memoirs, *Mandate for Change*, from which an excerpt is reprinted in this chapter. In this selection, Eisenhower recalls his early concerns as president, one of the first and most important of them being his State of the Union message to Congress. But his attempts to reduce the deficit while maintaining a strong national defense system and lowering taxes encountered serious difficulties.

Despite Eisenhower's continued dedication to conservative views, his desire to change the relationship between individuals and government in the United States, he failed to undo the New Deal. Faced with a potential global Cold War, a multiplying population, two serious recessions, and the complex problems arising from a modern industrial–urban society, Eisenhower was not only forced away from his original intent but by the end of his two terms in office he had essentially strengthened the New Deal and thus legitimized it. The evolution of the change which began to manifest itself in the middle of his first administration is succinctly treated by Professor Eric Goldman in his colorful book, *The Crucial Decade — And After*.

The Republican President's actions were bitterly decried by conservatives within his own party. While still deferring to his strength and popularity, conservatives were busy organizing on the local levels and turning to other figures to lead them out of the New Deal land. The rejection of Eisenhower could be best seen in an editorial in one of the most influential of conservative journals, the *National Review*, an organ established by William Buckley. The editorial was an assessment of Eisenhower's role as president. Entitled "So Long, Ike," it read in part:*

> The American people will do anything for a good man. Dwight Eisenhower is manifestly that. And if it had been he running for President last November, he'd have reduced Jack Kennedy to political dust in six speeches, syntax or no syntax. Indeed, no one could have run against Ike and beaten him . . . such a man, to his eternal credit, is Dwight Eisenhower. A man one can trust to do the good, according to his lights. And yet it must be said, what a miserable president he was . . . . Under

* *National Review* (January 14, 1961), 8–90

Eisenhower the forces that gnaw at the strength of our country grew stronger — the bureaucratic parasites, the labor union monopolists, the centralizers. He resisted some of the more radical impulses of the totalists, but his resistance was so theoretically anemic as to leave us disarmed. When the time came to defend ourselves against those who would push us further towards Socialism, all we had to offer was the mechanical reincarnation of Mr. Eisenhower's Progressive Moderation, Mr. Nixon. Oh Lord!

If the conservatives hoped to salvage part of Eisenhower's original moderate program through Richard Nixon, they were again to be bitterly disappointed, for he was defeated in 1960 in one of the closest of all presidential elections by John F. Kennedy. President Kennedy immediately began to expand on the New Deal program with his own New Frontier. It is no wonder that the conservatives began furiously to organize after the election of 1960 and to lay the groundwork for a revival of an earlier America. The results of their efforts can be seen in the powerful ultra-conservative movements of the 1960's.*

The Opposition of a Conservative Republican (1948) †

Senator Robert A. Taft

I listened yesterday with great interest to the President of the United States on the state of the union. The message states in general terms the ideals and principles and program of the present Administration. The detailed specifications for some actions have been already filled in by measures proposed, or presumably will be filled in by later messages.

No one can fail to agree with most of the ideals expressed by the President. No one can fail to agree with his general desire to bring about improved conditions in this country and throughout the world. No one can fail to agree with the five goals which he seeks. We all join with him in wishing the country a happy new year and a happy new ten years, happier than the fifteen years of New Deal administration.

But when the President comes to fill out the methods by which he hopes to accomplish this happiness and these great purposes, while he

---

* For a fuller explanation and analysis of the ultra-conservative movements, see Robert Rosenstone's book in this series, *Protest from the Right*.

† A transcript of a radio speech made on Thursday, January 8, 1948, by Senator Taft. From the *New York Times* (January 9, 1948), 6. Copyright 1948 by The New York Times Company. Reprinted by permission of the *Times*, and of Robert Taft, Jr., for the Estate of Robert A. Taft, Sr.

still speaks in general terms, we can see that under the guise of American ideals the old New Deal has been revived in a more global form than ever before. In this picture, the federal government comes forward again as Santa Claus himself, with a rich present for every special group in the United States, and for everyone else who may not be included in any special group.

If anyone has expressed a desire in a letter to Santa Claus, that desire is to be promptly fulfilled.

One cannot but feel that the recent announcement of Mr. Henry Wallace has had a substantial effect on the state of the union. Henry himself will have a hard time to find anything to promise the people of this country which is not promised in this message.

The President is apparently determined that the left wing of the American Labor Party and its labor-union friends throughout the country shall be bound to him and shall have no excuse to stray into the Wallace camp. He has raised all the ghosts of the old New Deal with new trappings that [Rexford G.] Tugwell and Harry Hopkins never thought of.

The first point that occurs to me is that the New Deal Administration has been in control of this government for fifteen years. If the country is crying for all these improvements in social welfare and every other field, what has the New Deal Administration been doing for fifteen years?

They demanded and obtained from Congress infinite power so great that President Roosevelt said it would only be safe in his hands and not in those of the Republicans. They demanded and received huge sums of money. Plenty of that money was spent, but apparently little was accomplished. The President admits it. He says our social security system has gaps and inconsistencies, and is only half finished.

As a matter of fact, the old-age insurance system is utterly and completely inadequate. Today, many who have contributed to that system all their lives receive less in their old age than many receive from old-age assistance who have contributed nothing.

The President says there is still "lack of provision for the nation's health," and that "most of our people cannot afford to pay for the care they need." This is a gross exaggeration, but what has the New Deal been doing with all our money?

He says that millions of children do not have adequate *school houses* or enough teachers, and that millions of our youth live in city slums and country shacks. Surely, this is a more severe indictment of the Roosevelt Administration than any Republican has made, for that Administration had more power and more money to accomplish its purposes, widely advertised for political effect, than any administration in the history of the United States.

Of course, the problem is not so simple as that. An improvement in social and economic welfare depends on intelligent planning, wise leadership, sound principles, and sound constructive work. Those we have not had.

Both parties—and Henry Wallace—wish to improve the condition of the people in the United States. That can be the only aim of anyone truly interested in government.

The Republican Party is just as much concerned as Mr. Truman with speeding up and stabilizing the great economic machine which creates prosperity for this country. It wishes to adopt those measures which will bring the greatest good to the greatest number of people, and then alleviate the condition of the few who, through misfortune, may not benefit from that prosperity.

There are few indeed in public life who have the slightest interest in whether a few rich men prosper or do not prosper, whether corporations make profits, or don't make profits, except as their status may affect the people of the country and the welfare of their employees. There are few indeed who don't equal the New Dealers in their sincere and earnest desire for uplift and progress in America. But we do question the effect of New Deal measures and philosophy.

Most of their plans are more likely to interfere with prosperity than they are to bring it about, first, because they ignore the fundamental economic principles necessary for prosperity; second, because they promise something for nothing, and, third, because they ignore the vital necessity of maintaining the principles of freedom and justice to which they give a general lip service.

Measures which destroy the freedom of the individual, freedom of states and local communities, freedom of the farmer to run his own farm and the workman to do his own job, in the end do more harm than good, even to those supposed to be benefited. Measures which reduce the field in which the free competition of private enterprise can operate, reduce both freedom and production. Measures which ignore justice for social ends destroy the fundamental purpose of the American government.

The first principle of the New Deal was the spending of money. This message, in tax recommendations, admits that taxation is already too heavy on millions of people. Yet strangely enough the message proposes additional expenditures, far beyond the $40 billion which is said to be included in the budget still to come. Nothing is said of additional taxation to take care of all the hand-outs that are proposed. The people are to get something for nothing from dear old Santa Claus.

What are these proposals likely to cost? They are so vague it is impossible to do more than make an intelligent guess. The level of benefits is to be raised for all unemployment compensation, old-age benefits, and survivors' benefits. In years to come this would amount to billions of dollars, mostly to be collected from employers, employees, and general taxation.

The national health-insurance system, which is not insurance at all, but the providing of free medical care to all the people of the United States, would require taxes, probably payroll taxes, in the neighborhood of $4 or $5 billion a year.

The President says: "Our ultimate aim must be a comprehensive insurance system to protect all our people equally against insecurity and ill health." This seems to be a kind of catch-all . . . plan . . . which would take about 18 per cent of payroll, or about $20 billion (including health insurance and present levies for old-age insurance and unemployment compensation). Of course it would be taxation, not insurance.

The various proposals for aid to education are vaguely stated, but I would guess they might amount to a billion dollars a year. The housing program might cost $200 million. From the message we cannot judge the estimate of the additional public works, but the reclamation program is to be expanded, although the Republican Congress in 1947 appropriated more money than has ever been appropriated before in a single year.

In some manner not defined, the average income of farmers is to be raised well above that which exists at present. Any such agricultural program as the President seems to envision will certainly take cash from the federal treasury in large hunks. More money is asked for the school-lunch program, the electrification program, the soil conservation program and adequate diets for every American family.

Then, in the field of foreign affairs, we come to the Marshall Plan involving about $3 billion a year more than we are now spending, but apparently included in this budget. The President states that we must maintain strong armed forces, and must add to our present system at least compulsory universal military training.

The cost of that is estimated anywhere from $2 billion to $4 billion.

The President's air commission is about to recommend an increase of $2 billion a year in the expenditures for our Air Force. If war with Russia is our present concern, then certainly the Air Force is going to play a much more effective part both in defending this country and attacking Russia than universal military training.

Altogether, I would estimate that if we follow the President's recommendations, we would spend almost at once $10 billion a year more than we are now spending, with later increases to come. Where is this money coming from? We raise today about $20 billion from the personal income tax. If we want to get the money from that personal tax, we will have to increase it by about 50 per cent.

Since you can't increase by 50 per cent the taxes of the wealthy, who pay 80 per cent already, most of the burden will have to fall on the lower and middle income groups. If the money is collected from more payroll taxes it will certainly fall on the lower incomes. If more business taxes and taxes on corporations are levied, they are paid in the last analysis by individuals, through higher prices or otherwise.

So in one way or another the 60 million workers in this country are going to pay those additional taxes, either directly or through further increases in prices.

In short, the President is simply following the old New Deal principle of promising the people something for nothing. No one has ever found out how that can be done. I do not mean to say that all the features of the President's program are to be condemned. I only point out that taken together they add up to national bankruptcy.

The President in some parts of his message compares the condition of our people favorably with 1938, incidentally in the midst of a New Deal depression. At other points he pictures the condition of our people as about equal to what prevails in Russia. What have we got for all the New Deal spending of the past fifteen years, except taxes and rising prices and war?

Now the President talks about a new ten-year plan, doubling Joe Stalin's bid. What reason have we to think that the social welfare of our people would improve any more in the next ten years than it has in the last fifteen years? The other feature of the message which stands out is the New Deal request for more power and more interference with the daily lives of the people.

The message asks again for rationing, for price control, for wage control, and for complete power to allocate the products of industry.

It asks again the power to draft 1.2 million boys a year out of their homes and schools and trades and professions into military training.

It asks again for power to socialize and nationalize medicine. Under the President's health program, $3 or $4 billion would pour into Washington in payroll taxes or other taxes to be used by a Washington bureau to pay all the doctors in the United States to give free medical service to all the people in the United States. That means, in effect, that all the doctors would become employees of the federal government.

It means that the government by regulation would determine when any family could have a doctor come to his home and when they would have to go to the clinic or the hospital, whether they could have X-ray treatments or special medicine, and the whole character of their medical treatment. Certainly, nothing could more intrude into the freedom of the American family than government medicine of this kind.

Throughout the message all the emphasis is on action by the federal government. Not a word is said anywhere of preserving the power of the state and local communities to improve their own affairs or direct their own education, health, welfare or housing. The message follows the standard New Deal line that places all power in Washington bureaus.

If we destroy the independence of our communities, I don't believe we can retain any popular freedom in a country the size of the United States. Again, I do not mean to condemn all of the projects. I only point out that, taken together, they will add up to a totalitarian state.

The ten-year Truman plan would leave about as much freedom in this country as Stalin's five-year plan has left in Russia.

Uncle Sam, Inc. (1950)*

Congressman Noah M. Mason

I was a guest in the Chicago Athletic Club some few years ago. That is probably one of the best equipped clubs in the country, if not in the world. I was sitting there in the Lounge Room admiring the magnificent furnishings, when I noticed a young man come out of the bowling alley, wiping the sweat from his forehead, and sit down beside an elderly gentleman who was reading the newspaper. Thinking to make conversation, I suppose, the young man said, "I'm a little stiff from bowling." And thinking to discourage conversation, I suppose, the elderly gentleman looked up from his newspaper and said, "Where did you say you were from?"

Well, I'm the little stiff from Washington that has come here to speak to you on "Uncle Sam, Inc.—The Biggest Business on Earth." It is a business that has been taking in something like $40 billion a year, and has been spending something like $40 or $50 billion a year. And, as a result, it is $300 billion in the red today. It's a business that has a Board of Directors numbering 531, the majority of whom believe in deficit spending, in spending more than they take in. It has a general manager, who lives in the White House. He also believes in spending

---

*From *Vital Speeches of the Day*, Vol. XVII, No. 5, pp. 143–46. This speech, by the full title of "Uncle Sam, Inc.—The Biggest Business on Earth," was given by the Illinois Congressman before the Economic Club of Detroit, Michigan on October 23, 1950. Opening and concluding paragraphs are eliminated here.

more than he takes in—deficit spending—because he is always urging and recommending and demanding that his board of directors do that very thing.

But this greatest corporation on earth, Uncle Sam, Inc., has 100 million stockholders entitled to vote, but less than half of them are interested enough in their business, the biggest business on earth, to bother to vote for either the board of directors or the general manager. Forty-eight million in 1948 voted. Fifty-two million in 1948 didn't bother to vote. And so these stockholders get about the kind and the caliber of members for their board of directors and their general manager that they deserve. No better and no worse. If these 100 million stockholders want their business, the biggest business on earth, run economically and efficiently, in the black and not in the red; then, they must take more interest in the business and do their part, at least, in selecting the best men they can find for that board of directors, and the most outstanding man in the country for general manager. And if they don't do that, they shouldn't grumble too much if the board of directors continues to squander and bungle, if they have to continue paying heavy taxes, if their boys are taken in uniform and sent 7,000 miles away, if they have regulations and controls that are irksome put upon them. They have no one to blame but themselves. And, November 7th is coming.

With that as an introduction, with that as a preface, I want you to keep that preface in mind while I give you three phases of this biggest business on earth: (1) Uncle Sam's Debt, (2) Uncle Sam's Expenditures, and (3) Uncle Sam's Tax System. I want to discuss each of those three phases very briefly with you. A kind of a bird's eye picture of each one of them.

What about Uncle Sam's debt? Treasury reports tell us that we are in the red to the tune of $257 billion, but those Treasury reports do not give you the full picture because Uncle Sam has other obligations not covered in the Treasury reports, amounting to something like $40 billion: obligations incurred by the Commodity Credit Corporation, the Export-Import Bank, the R.F.C., the International Bank, the International Fund, and several other loaning agencies. And so today Uncle Sam, Inc.—and that means you and I—owes something like $300 billion.

I don't know what $300 billion is. You don't know. The finite mind can't grasp such an astronomical sum as that. But I do know that Uncle Sam today owes more than all of our allies in the last war put together: England, France, Italy, Russia, China and the forty–odd other countries that go to make up the United Nations organization; more than all of them put together owe. And yet, we have the spectacle today of practically every nation on earth standing in front of Uncle Sam with her hands out, saying in effect, "Please, Uncle Sam, your credit is still good. Won't you borrow more money? Won't you go deeper into debt? Won't you levy heavier taxes upon your people and help us out of the mess that we're in?" And Uncle Sam has been doing that. He is doing that. And his board of directors proposes to continue to do that.

Fifty-some-odd billion dollars lend-lease during the war. Forty billion since that time. And a large part of that lend-lease, $11 billion, went to Russia during the war, and a large part of the $40 billion since has gone to Russia, siphoned there through her satellite nations. Now, we're proposing to continue the Marshall Plan, to spend billions to rearm Europe, not to say anything about the President's Point IV Program. Where is it going to end? In my opinion it can only end in one way: financial chaos, national bankruptcy, repudiation and then dictatorship. Unless your board of directors makes a right about-face and stops this shoveling out, that is where we are sure to end. That is the picture so far as Uncle Sam's debt is concerned.

Now, what about Uncle Sam's expenditures? Well, the President sent his budget message up to the Congress last January, and in that budget message he asked for about $42.5 billion to operate this nation during this present financial year. That was some budget message. In size and shape it resembled a Sears Roebuck catalogue. It was two inches thick. It weighed six pounds. It had 1,198 pages in it, enumerating thousands of items. But that budget message and that budget can be boiled down, it can be analyzed, it can be condensed, into six general items. I want to place those six general items in front of you so that you will get a picture of our expenditures.

Item No. 1. What is that? Interest on the national debt. How much? Five billion, six hundred million dollars. How much is $5.6 billion? Well, it is more than Uncle Sam ever took in in any one year in his life, up until 1940. It is more than the United States ever spent in one peacetime year in his life up until the New Deal took over. And now it is going for one item alone, Interest on the national debt.

What's Item No. 2? National defense. How much? Fifteen billion dollars. When I first went to Congress, the first six years I was there, we appropriated about a billion dollars a year for national defense. Half a billion for the Army and half a billion for the Navy. Now, $15 billion, five years after the war is over. Why? Why? Well, some of our officials say it is to pay for the Cold War we're in. That's a superficial answer. This is my answer: It is to pay for the mistakes our leaders made at Yalta, at Teheran, at Cairo, and at Potsdam. Rather expensive mistakes. We have been in a Cold War for five years trying to contain

Communism. During that five years, Stalin, who was a dictator over 300 million Russians during World War II, has spread his—I was going to say wings—claws, talons, over 600 million more people. That means that he is dictator today over 900 million people. That's how successful we have been in this Cold War of ours.

Stalin today has surrounded himself with satellite nations, puppet nations, iron curtain nations—whatever you want to call them—and he sits in Moscow like a big fat spider in the center of his web. He pulls a string in Korea and war breaks out, and we send our fire brigade over there to put out the flames of war, at a cost of $3 or $4 billion. When that is over—and it will be over pretty soon—he can and he will pull another string in Indo-China, or in India, or in Siam, or in Berlin, or in Turkey, or in Greece, or in Yugoslavia. And then we will have to send our fire brigade again and spend billions more to put that fire out. And after three or four years of that kind of a thing we will be exhausted, bled white. He won't have needed to have lost a man of his own. And then we will be in a mess, and that's what our thinkers are finally beginning to sense.

Let's get back to these budget items. That was Item No. 2. What is Item No. 3? Veterans' benefits. How much? Six billion dollars. Most of you can remember the bonus march, and the bonus that was put across over the President's veto. You can remember that the President said, in paying that $3.5 to $4 billion bonus, that it would bankrupt the nation. Well, we're spending twice that much each year now for veterans' benefits, and worrying very little about bankrupting the nation. We ought to do a little more worrying about it.

Item No. 4. What is that? International relief, the Marshall Plan, rearming, and so forth and so on. How much? Six billion dollars. That also is a part of the cost of the mistakes our leaders made at Yalta, and at Teheran, and at Potsdam, and so forth.

Item No. 5. Federal payroll. How much? Six and one-half billion dollars. Fourteen years ago when I went to Congress our annual payroll was about $1.5 billion. We had between 600 and 700 thousand people on the federal payroll then. Now we have over 2 million. Times have changed! Can we reduce that expenditure for that item, federal payroll? Well, Senator Byrd has been saying for ten years, that I know of, that we can cut it in half and get better work done and more work done by getting rid of the dead timber on the payroll. And I agree with him. And the Hoover Commission came up a couple of years ago with the same report, the same answer that Byrd has been offering to us. Will we do it? No, we won't, under our present board of directors. Why not? I'll let you in on a secret. The scarcest thing in Washington today is not brains, it's backbone, it's courage, it's guts. The scarcest thing in Washington today! We respond to this pressure and that pressure, and that pressure, from these pressure groups, instead of doing what we were elected to do, and that is, taking the nation as a whole and doing what is best for the nation. That will be the situation until we change our board of directors —yes, and our general manager, because he still has the veto power, and it takes a lot of votes to get across that veto power. We do it once in a while, with the help of good American Democrats—and we have some.

What is Item No. 6, the last one? I'll lump them up and call it a miscellaneous item. It amounts to $3.5 billion. What is it? Oh, subsidies of all kinds, and federal aid to the states, of all kinds; school lunches— $100 million because the people of America can't afford to feed their children today and Uncle Sam has to do it for them.

And a lot of other nonsense, amounting to $42.5 billion, but that isn't the whole picture of our expenditures.

Well, what is the rest of it? Four or five other items that the President has been urging and recommending and demanding over the past four or five years that would cost at least $25 billion to $30 billion more on top of that $42.5 billion. What are they? Universal military training: $3 billion. I'm coming around to the belief that we must have that now. What else? The Brannan Plan to socialize and control American agriculture. How much? $6 billion to $8 billion, at a conservative estimate. What else? Compulsory health insurance. Call it what you will, it is still socialized medicine. How much? At least $6 billion to $8 billion; at least that much. What else? A full employment program, with unemployment insurance payments from $30 per week to $42 per week, depending upon your dependents—by the way, that is Scott Lucas' bill; it's Senate 3427 —for twenty-six weeks; that is, six months. When they put it across, and I'm a colored gentleman in the South with a family of five or six or seven children, not liking to work very well, I work for a month or so, then I take six months on big pay, unemployment compensation—bigger than I can earn—and go fishing and hunting and doing what I please. That's the picture, and that is what we are facing. Full employment: every man guaranteed a job, and when he hasn't got a job, whether it is his fault or somebody else's fault, he receives $30 to $42 per week.

Think what that will mean.

That is the picture, as I see it, of Uncle Sam's expenditures. Add that $20 to $30 billion to your $42.5 billion, and see that you "ain't seen nothing yet" so far as your taxes are concerned.

Let's take the third part, Uncle Sam's tax system. Of course, I deal with that. That is my province in the Ways and Means Committee. That's what I came to Michigan about sixteen years ago. It was before

I was in Congress. That was when I was in the [Illinois] State Senate and came up here to advise the Michigan Legislature. I spoke to both Houses on the tax system of Illinois and what they should do in Michigan. What about Uncle Sam's tax system? Well, our federal tax rates today are confiscatory. They have passed the point of diminishing returns. They are drying up the streams of investment capital. They are placing handicaps upon business expansion. And they have made it impossible for any new business to start up with any hope of success, under our tax rates. Every large business in the nation today grew up before our tax rates became confiscatory. Think that through. Whenever you take the major part of a profit dollar from a big manufacturer you take away his incentive to expand, to create more jobs, to produce more goods for the hungry consuming public. That's what you do. I have always said that tax rates and jobs are Siamese twins. They are tied together. They are closely related. You just can't separate them. I defy anybody to deny this. Under normal conditions—not war conditions—whenever you have high tax rates you always have a contracting national economy, fewer jobs, smaller payrolls, more unemployment, and less production. Whenever you have low tax rates you have an expanding economy, more jobs, more employment, no unemployment—or very little—and higher production; always they go together under normal conditions.

Whenever you take from 25 to 30 per cent of the average taxpayer's income, as you are doing today, you are placing too heavy a burden upon the average taxpayer. You are making him work from three to four months a year for the government, and eight to nine months for himself and his family. Whenever you take 80 to 90 cents out of every dollar of the high income bracket chap, as you are doing today, you're "killing the goose that lays the golden eggs." The golden eggs in this instance being jobs, employment, production and so forth. That is the picture you have today.

Let me give you an example. In 1945 the Congress passed a tax reduction bill reducing taxes something like $6 to $7 billion. The President signed that tax reduction bill—that was President Truman, too—in the face of a $21 billion deficit that year. The major part of that tax reduction was in the repeal of the excess profits tax. (I have to go back on November 1 and try to draft another one to take its place.) Repeal of the excess profits tax; what happened? Well, the $4 billion-odd that was being paid in to Uncle Sam's Treasury by this excess profits tax, by big business, was retained by big business and ploughed back into plant expansion. That's what happened. Now, what were the results. A business boom happened. Five million three hundred thousand new jobs were created. We reached an all-time peak of employment—that 60 million mark that F.D.R. said we would reach in 1950, and we reached it two years ahead of time.

What else happened? The national index of production went up 15 points. We produced a lot more. Normally and naturally the prices would have fallen on these goods, but we shipped to Europe that year $14 billion worth of goods—mostly scarce goods: steel, farm machinery, tractors, food, and the like—and so the prices didn't fall.

What else happened? As Ripley says, "believe it or not," we took more dollars into the United States Treasury after the tax reduction bill than we had been taking before, and in 1948 we actually had a balance of $8.4 billion in the Treasury. We applied $5 billion on the national debt. We earmarked $3 billion-odd for the Marshall Plan. Now, believe it or not, that was the result of that tax reduction bill. And, under Mellon, after the First World War, we had four tax reduction programs and the same thing resulted each time. That is logic, economics, business, that most of our Administration leaders don't seem to grasp or know anything about. We're due for a change, and if the stockholders don't wake up and see to it that we get a change, they deserve what they get.

I could go on. I can say this: that before the war the American public used to save 15 to 20 per cent of their national income and reinvest it in expanding American business; now, we save less than 6 per cent of our bloated national income—our 40-cent dollars, or whatever they are—and so the streams of investment capital are being dried up. That is the situation.

I have given you a picture of Uncle Sam's debts; I have given you a picture of Uncle Sam's expenditures—bird's eye picture; and a picture of his tax system, that is badly in need of doctoring up.

Now what can I say? I want to say something in closing. What are you going to do about it? I have painted the picture. What are you going to do about it? And when I say "you," I mean not only these people here, but other people all over this nation. Do you fellows know that out of a hundred top business executives in Chicago alone—a survey was made—eighty-four were registered to vote in the 1948 election; forty-four out of the hundred voted. And yet no one screams louder than those business executives about the tax load and about things as they are going on. Do they deserve what they get? I imagine there are maybe one or two in this group that didn't vote in the 1948 election. November 7 is coming. I could go on and give you a lot of figures on those stay-at-home votes. Fifty-two million out of the 100 million didn't vote last time. You deserve about what you get. What do we need today? We need a revival of Americanism and patriotism; the kind of Americanism

VERNON REGIONAL
JUNIOR COLLEGE LIBRARY

and patriotism that inspired our revolutionary fathers—the boys in blue and the boys in grey; the patriotism that carried them through Chateau-Thierry and the Anzio beachhead and Iwo Jima and the rest of it. That is the kind of patriotism we need. Tom Paine said during the Revolutionary War, in describing the crisis that faced the nation then, "These are the times that try men's souls. The summer soldier and the sunshine patriot will in this crisis shrink from his duty; but he that stands it now deserves the love and praise of men and women." We have too many summer soldiers and sunshine patriots in America today, who accept the good things of citizenship and the privileges of citizenship but they shirk their duty and responsibility of citizenship.

The Socialist Party Platform of 1948*

Preamble

Mankind is haunted by new fears. In the crowded metropolis and on the distant farm, men ask themselves whether, under freedom, depression can be avoided, poverty vanquished and war uprooted.

Starvation stalks much of the world, and in our own land men dread the insecurity that tomorrow may bring. While millions go in rags, the world's looms are again knitting the uniforms that will shroud new victims to be offered on the altars of nationalism, imperialism, and tyranny.

In 1948, we face the elemental question of survival. The atomic revolution has burst upon the world and a new unity has been forged among the human race: men who have refused to be brothers one of another may now become children of a common doom.

—Unless we learn to reorganize our society for survival and not for mutual extinction;

—Unless we learn new techniques of cooperation to replace the old policies of competition;

—Unless we move rapidly toward socialization by which alone the individual can be preserved in the inter-dependent world of the turbine, the plane, the steel mill and the uranium pile;

—Unless we move rapidly to a world order without greed, profit, and hate.

The American people, because of the accidents of geography, will make the decision for mankind. Our mines and factories were not

---

* From *National Party Platforms*, Kirk H. Porter and Donald Bruce Johnson, eds. (Urbana, Illinois: University of Illinois Press, 1966), pp. 454–58.

devastated by the physical havoc of the last war. For America, and consequently the world, it is not too late.

Three forces today are competing for the loyalty of men. And in this race, the stakes are the survival of mankind.

On one hand, an economic system calling itself "free enterprise" asserts that it can lead to the salvation of humanity. It has brought us repeatedly to depressions and wars, yet its spokesmen in the Democratic and Republican Parties still pretend they have solutions.

They have, in fact, betrayed the promises with which they woo the American people every four years. They offered prosperity and delivered depression. They pledged peace and delivered war. They promised to increase our standard of living and are now raising the cost of living. They promised freedom to organized labor and hobbled it with new bonds.

They have sought partisan advantage and jeopardized national welfare. The dominant wings in their parties have combined to destroy price control and give us inflation, to undermine restraints on greed and give us shortage, to favor the rich and deny the poor, to cut the taxes of the wealthy and insult the common man with a crumb.

There is a second force in the world—which promises security and speaks of freedom but delivers only economic bondage and dictatorship. It is the force of totalitarianism. Yesterday its most sinister front was Fascism; today it is Communism.

In the United States, it marches under masked banners. It calls itself a "new party" and has pushed into the forefront well-meaning liberals who do not know the purposes of their Communist allies. And this alliance, though speaking for civil liberties at home, defends the most powerful tyranny in the modern world. It speaks of peace but is blind to the most aggressive imperialism of the present day. It speaks of one world but works for two spheres of influence. It urges the brotherhood of man but sanctifies the divisive principle of national sovereignty.

As against these forces, the Socialist Party of the United States speaks for the Third Force—democratic socialism, the principles of democratic planning and international order. This socialist program for the United States today includes these major goals:

Basic Socialist Demands

1) The natural resources of the nation—minerals, oil, electric and atomic power—are the property of the people. Their preservation for future generations and their management by the people for social purposes can be achieved democratically under socialism.

2) The basic industries, public utilities, banking and credit institutions—all the economic facilities needed for the satisfaction of the fun-

damental requirements of the people—must be socially owned and democratically managed.

3) Socialism will democratize the economic life of the nation by the joint representation of workers, the working management, and the consuming public, in the management of socialized enterprises; by the guarantee of popular control of enterprise through the maximum decentralization economically feasible and the use of various types of organization, particularly the public corporation and the voluntary cooperative; and by the preservation of the freedom of labor organization and of consumer choice.

With such control we can have democratic planning. The lessons of the last war have taught that only by planning, by large-scale government investment, by decisive national action, can production be increased to meet the goals set by the nation. In place of the destructive ends sought in wartime, the nation must now fix its peacetime goals—food for the ill-fed, clothing for the ill-clothed, homes for the ill-housed.

A nation that could fill the skies with planes and the oceans with warships can fill its streets and avenues with homes, schools, and hospitals; swell its granaries and storehouses; bring joy to its people and the world. In the light of this Socialist program for democratic planning, we offer this platform to the American people in the 1948 elections. It can be achieved.

Domestic Program

1) *Raise the Standard of Living*

It must be the constant task of the nation to raise the standard of living of its people. This can be effected only by a continually rising trend in production and wage levels, the stabilization of prices, and the immediate elimination of profits as the determining factor in production. In a period of inflation wage increases without price controls are delusions.

2) *Expand the Productive Facilities of the Nation*

The American standard of living and the needs of world economic rehabilitation make it essential that our national production be rapidly expanded. An economy based on profit will not expand so long as scarcity is profitable and inflation an easy road to gain.

The Socialist Party calls for government action to assure investment in new plant capacity through the establishment of public corporations for the production of ever-mounting quantities of steel, oil and other raw materials, and the utilization of the nation's water resources for the development of cheaper and more abundant electric power. A far-flung program of Tennessee Valley Administrations, Missouri Valley Administrations and Rural Electrification Administration cooperatives can effect the electrification of whole areas that are lagging far behind their agricultural and industrial potential. Only by planned growth in our national output of civilian goods can we end the menace of inflation, which is now dangerously increased by our enormous expenditures on arms.

3) Expand Social Legislation

The intricacies of twentieth-century living and the potentialities of modern technology have at last made it possible to guarantee a national minimum standard of living for the population. The Socialist Party advocates:

a. Expansion of unemployment insurance and social security. Millions of workers are as yet uncovered by the unemployment and social security provisions. The present law discriminates against farm labor, domestic servants, and other working groups despite the Constitutional guarantee of the "equal protection of the laws." Even so, the Democratic-Republican coalition in Congress has been whittling down the number of workers protected by the existing law at a time when extension of coverage should be the order of the day.

The age at which workers become eligible for old age pensions should be promptly reduced to 60, and the system should be financed by net progressive income taxation rather than by the regressive payroll tax. The benefits—now drastically cut by the current inflation—should be raised.

The Social Security law should be amended to include family allowances. The proper care of children is at least as important as the care of the aged.

b. Minimum wage. The present legal minimum wage under the Wage-Hour Law should be immediately raised to the 75 cents an hour demanded by organized labor, with progressive increases to occur periodically.

The number of employees protected by the Act must be increased by a redefinition of coverage; and the present reactionary drive to reduce the coverage must be defeated.

c. Health services. Legislation for comprehensive medical and hospital care, financed by a national contributory system of health insurance, must be enacted by Congress. The Democratic-Republican coalition has successfully blocked the health insurance bill. In contrast, the Taft health bill will not provide comprehensive medical care nor remove the economic barriers now depriving millions of proper medical service.

Only a national health insurance program can guarantee free access to medical care, freedom of doctors' choice, and freedom for the medical profession within a framework of public responsibility.

Neither a fee-for-service system nor voluntary prepayment plans can bring the benefits of modern medical science to all the people, regardless of race, color, creed, geography, or economic condition.

Federal tax funds should be used to supplement an insurance program in creating a fully rounded national health service.

Public health services must be increased; the construction of new hospitals and clinics must be pushed. Federal action must be taken to stimulate research and public preventive medicine in cancer, heart diseases, mental illness, alcoholism, and other ailments, as was done in the field of atomic fission. The maternal and child services provided by the Social Security Act must be extended.

d. *Education.* It is a national disgrace that the richest nation in the world does not have the best possible educational program from the nursery school to the university. America has subjected its children and youth to a shameful chronic emergency in this field. Higher standards of teacher training, enlarged and improved facilities, curricula better designed to meet pupil needs, adequate salaries, attractive conditions for superior professional work—all require that federal contributions to public education be vastly multiplied without reducing local community initiative and existing state responsibilities.

At the same time, legislative efforts to divert public funds to private sectarian schools must be defeated. The principle of separation of church and state must be consistently applied in the use of public educational funds.

We propose passage of state and federal laws aimed at eliminating racial, cultural, and religious discrimination and segregation in education.

e. *Veterans.* Because of the special hardships war worked upon the veterans and conscientious objectors, we favor legislation to provied them substantial and adequate benefits in the form of education, medical care and loans; and full care for the families of those who did not return. We demand immediate steps to end the vicious discrimination and outright fraud now being practiced against Negro, Nisei, Spanish- or Mexican-American veterans by prejudiced local employees of the Veterans Administration, particularly in the South and Southwest.

4) *Expand the Nation's Housing Facilities*

Private enterprise has failed dismally to meet the challenge of housing the American people. Its boast that the lifting of controls on new construction would stimulate large-scale building has proved hollow.

The lower income groups most desperately in need of housing, the young people—particularly our veterans—and the inhabitants of our ever-growing slums, are not in a position to buy or rent the facilities that private contractors are willing or able to erect. . . .

The Socialist Party proposes the creation of a Home Loan Bank to finance the purchase of homes, a Public Supply and Fabricating Corporation to set up factory units needed to produce materials and to develop large-scale prefabricated housing: the expansion of public housing activities in the field of low-income multiple dwellings; the expansion of publicly built, cooperative tenant-operated housing; the integration of national and local housing plans, including revision of municipal building codes; the development of a government program of bona fide collective bargaining with the building and construction unions, providing for a guaranteed annual wage to remove one of the worst evils of the building industry and for the development of apprentice-training programs.

We favor the extension and strengthening of rent control for the duration of the housing emergency. The people of America must call to account those legislators who are destroying rent controls, permitting eviction of tenants by subterfuge and so contributing to disastrous inflation in the field of housing.

5) Protect the Nation's Title to Atomic Energy Pending Internationalization
The United States has made a good beginning in reserving to the nation, rather than ceding to business, the ownership of atomic energy. But this principle is already being undermined by cost-plus contracts, granted to private corporations to exploit this new storehouse of power for profit as coal, oil, and other resources have been in the past. Nuclear fission was not the product of private enterprise. It was financed by the nation and was achieved by cooperative scientific effort operating in complete disregard of the profit motive. As the peace-time uses of atomic energy begin to emerge, it becomes increasingly important that the constructive applications of atomic power be utilized only through non-profit public corporations.

6) Strengthen Civil and Political Liberties
Civil and political liberties are in serious danger today. The Socialist Party calls for greater vigilance and specifically demands:

a. Repeal of the Taft-Hartley Act which undermines the right to strike, the right to organize, the right to sign contracts guaranteeing union security and furthering the economic interests of organized workers; and which permits the power of the state to be used in behalf of employers and against workers with just grievances. The Socialist Party pledges its full support to organized labor in its effort to repeal the Taft-Hartley Act and similar state laws.

b. Elimination of the Committee on Un-American Activities which has pursued the dishonest tradition of the Dies Committee. The Committee has abused the legitimate democratic function of Congress to investigate and collect data on matters of national importance.

c. Defeat of any legislation that would force the Communist Party further underground and that would appear to give moral justification to its conspiratorial policies. The right to free expression of political views must not be impaired. But the existing laws against overt acts should be vigorously enforced.

d. Elimination of poll taxes and opening of the ballot to citizens regardless of income.

e. Full amnesty and restoration of civil rights for war objectors, several hundred of whom are still in prison and thousands of whom have lost citizenship.

7) *Establish Racial Equality*

Democracy cannot tolerate two classes of citizenship. Complete political, economic and social equality, regardless of race, religion, or national origin, must be established.

a. Segregation must be abolished in the armed forces, in all public institutions, and in housing.

b. Legislation for a Fair Employment Practices Committee, long overdue, should be passed.

c. Anti-lynching legislation must be enacted to wipe out the worst blot on the American scene.

d. Naturalization rights should be granted to Japanese immigrants who have demonstrated their loyalty, and indemnification should be given to Japanese immigrants and their American descendants who suffered property losses because of government policy during World War II.

e. All forms of discriminating barriers against immigration on grounds of race, color, or national origin must be abolished.

f. Guarantee the right to vote to many citizens now robbed of suffrage. The 14th Amendment of the Constitution, depriving states of representation in Congress in proportion to the number of citizens deprived of the right to vote by virtue of race, color, or previous condition of servitude, should be promptly enforced.

8) *Safeguard American Agriculture*

The Socialist Party opposes the absentee ownership of farms and its attendant tenancy in America. We reaffirm our position that occupancy and use should be the only rightful title to farmland. Where conditions favor family farming, the security of such farmers should be strength-ened through cooperative credit purchasing and marketing, aided by government financing. Where modern techniques and specialization re-quire large-scale farm enterprises, we call for social ownership and co-operative operation to replace the corporation farm which threatens both the security and freedom of farm workers.

We disapprove of the New Deal idea of agricultural scarcity, aimed at keeping prices up by limiting production. Our domestic needs and those of the world require an agricultural program based on maximum production.

We urge the continuation and expansion of the present conservation program to check destruction by floods, erosion of topsoil, and depletion of farm fertility. Our obligation to our grandchildren demands a greater concern with the heritage we leave in productive farmland.

The proper distribution and marketing of food and fiber does not require gambling. Our present Board of Trade pricing of farm produce, with its poker-game practices of buying on futures, must be ended.

9) *Establish a Progressive Tax System*

The Tax Law of 1948 is legislation for the direct and immediate benefit of the wealthiest group in the country. Their taxes have been drastically lowered without any real assurance that corresponding eco-nomic benefits in the form of additional equity capital for new produc-tion will result. The tax reduction for those in the lower income brackets is petty, and will disappear altogether after November if a Democratic or Republican Congress is elected.

We propose:

a. Raising the present exemption levels to equal the amounts neces-sary to sustain minimum standards of living.

b. Restoring the earned Income Credit in such form that it grants a tax benefit (with an appropriate maximum) to income from wages and salary in contrast to income from investment.

c. Tightening of the provisions of the Estate Tax section of the Internal Revenue Code by increasing the rates, lowering the exemption, and plugging the loop-holes by which inherited wealth can be passed on for two and sometimes more generations, by means of trusts, without paying succession taxes. Corresponding changes must be made in the Gift Tax section.

d. Modification of the Internal Revenue Code's favored treatment of speculative and gambling profits, and encouragement of new equity capital for production by revision of the treatment of Capital Assets.

e. Financing of extraordinary government expenses through a capital levy, especially on the increase in private capital since 1939, so that those who benefited directly from World War II will bear the burden of the nation's war deficit.

f. We condemn the fraudulent joint-return provision of the new tax law as a device which enables the wealthy to minimize their share of the tax burden.

10) Financing the Socialist Program

The American people will be told that it is impossible to finance this program for economic security. The cost of World War II to the American people was some 350 billion dollars. It is fantastic to assert that we cannot afford to devote a fraction of that sum to the peace and happiness of the nation. On the basis of the program submitted to Congress by the Armed Forces, it is apparent that our military budget alone in 1952 will equal the present total national budget. The path to plenty lies in expanding our production and in reallocating our budget in the service of life and peace.

Mandate for Change (1963)*

Dwight D. Eisenhower

Many other matters, large and small, crowded the ensuing days, but of all these the most urgent was that of preparing a suitable State of the Union message, which, after arranging the date with congressional leaders, I was to deliver on February 2 [1953].

With the chance for new policies and ideas to come into the federal government after twenty years of another philosophy, I wanted to make it clear that we would not be simply a continuation of the New Deal and Fair Deal, either in purpose or execution.

"Our industrial plant is built," Franklin D. Roosevelt declared in a famous speech in 1932, when the United States had a gross national product of $58 billion—less than 30 per cent (in constant dollars) of what it is today. And he went on,

> The problem just now is whether under existing conditions it is not overbuilt. Our last frontier has long since been reached. . . .

---

* From *The White House Years: Mandate for Change: 1953–1956*, by Dwight D. Eisenhower. Copyright © 1963 by Dwight D. Eisenhower. Reprinted by permission of Doubleday & Company, Inc.

> Our task now is not discovery or exploitation of natural resources or necessarily producing more goods. It is the soberer, less dramatic business of administering resources and plants already in hand . . . of distributing wealth and products more equitably. . . .

I did not share the belief that the American economy was overbuilt; that parceling out scarcities was the way to economic justice; that the federal government had to establish a rigid economic order for the whole country; that only a Niagara of federal spending could power the country's ecomonic progress; and that, all other things being equal, the federal government deserved first opportunity and had the right to solve any major problem that might arise in the nation.

In initiating a reversal of trends based on such beliefs—trends which by 1953 were twenty years old—we were setting in motion revolutionary activity. We suffered no delusion that such a revolution could become a reality through the frenzied drama of a first one hundred days, or that it could be the work of improvisation, however clever.

I therefore wanted to outline in the State of the Union message the philosophy of the new Administration.

This message would be one of my most important pronouncements of policy; in every possible way I sought information, opinions, and advice on every subject that I thought might appropriately be included. During the twelve days between my inauguration and the delivery of the talk I made it the principal subject of two Cabinet and one National Security Council meetings. Among the many I saw was Senator Taft, with whom I had a long talk on reduction of federal expenditures and plans for the removal of governmental controls over the economy. As before, we were in substantial agreement as to principle.

In spite of study and research I was not certain that the message achieved exactly the tone I desired; possibly it contained too many details. I find in my files a note expressing my feelings, written on the morning of February 2:

> Today I give my first "State of the Union" talk before a Joint Session of the Congress. I feel it is a mistake for a new Administration to be talking so soon after inauguration; basic principle, expounded in an inaugural talk is one thing — but to begin talking concretely about a great array of specific problems is quite another. Time for study, exploration, and analysis is necessary. But — the Republicans have been so long out of power they want and probably need — a pronouncement from their President as a starting point. This I shall try to give. I hope — and pray — that it does not contain blunders that we will later regret.

At noon that day, having reached the Capitol and met an escorting committee of members from both houses, I proceeded with them to the entrance of the chamber of the House of Representatives and heard the doorkeeper, Tom Kennamer, call out, "Mr. Speaker, the President of the United States!" (It was the first time in our century—possibly in our history—when a President, preparing to deliver his first State of the Union message, could recall that this was the second time he had addressed a joint session of Congress. The first occasion was when I came back, temporarily, to the United States shortly after V-E Day in 1945.)

The principles of the message echoed those I had expounded during the political campaign just completed. They had as a backdrop the dark international reality outlined in the Inaugural Address—the recognition that the "forces of good and evil are massed and armed and opposed as rarely before in history," that "freedom is pitted against slavery, lightness against the dark."

Assuming these facts, I announced at the outset of the message these four aims:

> Application of America's influence in world affairs with such fortitude and such foresight that it will deter aggression and eventually secure peace;
>
> Establishment of a national administration of such integrity and such efficiency that its honor at home will ensure respect abroad;
>
> Encouragement of those incentives that inspire creative initiative in our economy, so that its productivity may fortify freedom everywhere; and
>
> Dedication to the well-being of all our citizens and to the attainment of equality of opportunity for all, so that our Nation will ever act with the strength of unity in every task in which it is called.

To others these may have been banal generalities. For me they were principles to which I intended to adhere.

.   .   .   .

After delivering the State of the Union message I returned to the White House. Within hours I was presiding over a meeting on bringing wage and price controls to an end.

On the day I delivered the State of the Union message there were price ceilings on millions of products in American stores—tens of thousands of little white tags listing the lawful upper price limit on products, as set by the Office of Price Stabilization. The OPS, with its Washington headquarters in temporary buildings on the Mall, had a web of regional and district offices, and more than ten thousand employees scattered all over the country futilely trying to keep the lid on the cost of items from toasters, irons, and frying pans to textiles, clothes, and gasoline. On that afternoon also, millions of American men and women were working under wage ceilings set by the Wage Stabilization Board, a body made up of four members from management, four from labor, and four from the "general public," with a stormy history of resignations, new appointments, and bad feelings.

The organizations, their bureaucratic methods, the ceiling prices, ceiling wages, price tags, compliance posters, and endless paper work had outlived their usefulness. We were determined to get rid of them.

There was no lack of dire predictions on what would happen if price controls were taken away. In May of 1952 President Truman had urged their continuation. At the height of the campaign that year a Democratic spokesman announced that 88 per cent of American housewives wanted controls kept on; he said they should be made even stronger. Accordingly, in the last days of the campaign, Governor Stevenson pledged "vigorous price controls" if the American people would elect him.

We rejected these views. But the question of how to remove controls remained. Should they meet quick and sudden death, as Secretary Humphrey and Secretary Wilson urged? Or should we extinguish them slowly, as Cabot Lodge and Harold Stassen recommended, to avoid skyrocketing prices? Arthur Flemming, Director of the Office of the Defense Mobilization, took a middle position: we should lift controls gradually, category by category, but soon. Decontrols should begin that very week. Wages should be decontrolled in one action, and so at the same time should the prices of many consumer goods, including meats, furniture, and textiles. This was the plan I decided to use. Four days later I signed Executive Order 10432, and wage controls—along with some price controls—were history.

Six days later, on February 12, Dr. Flemming presented proposals for further decontrols. After a discussion in which Joseph Dodge warned that price rises would increase defense costs, and Foster Dulles reminded us that a worsening of the international situation might require the reimposition of controls, I remarked to the Cabinet that we could not live our lives under emergency measures and anticipated economic eruptions. Then I directed the decontrol of another group of items, including crude rubber, soap, poultry, lead, and glass. Controls on other items— among them tobacco, coal, and farm machinery—were to remain for a brief time, and controls on critical defense items for as long as necessary. We supported legislation to keep rent controls on until the state legislatures could deal with the problem.

The Administration was not going to rigidly follow economic doctrine regardless of human hardship. I warned the Congressional leaders at one meeting that we must always keep uppermost our concern for the individual, because "economic laws are sometimes slow to operate" and people can get hurt.

On the morning of March 5 I could tell the press that "I have been gratified to see that there has been little discernible evidence that anyone is trying to gouge, or take advantage of the situation." Prices were holding steady. They continued to hold remarkably steady through the Administration's eight years. In 1951 Winston Churchill based his comeback campaign—victoriously—on the slogan "Set the People Free." In February 1953, with the sweeping away of economic controls, we had begun to do just that in the United States.

Now the Administration (familiar with the history of the control system, which during its lifetime had seemed to be less a lid clamped on a boiling pot than an express elevator headed for the roof) deliberately took on the heavy responsiblity of watching closely every economic indicator and of being ready to take any action necessary to strengthen the country's economic health. One of the most significant of these indicators is the consumer price index—which shows what consumers are paying for goods and services now by comparison with what they paid at a fixed date in the past.

Between 1945 and 1952 the consumer price index had gone up nearly 50 per cent; the value of the dollar went down more than 33 per cent. The price of children's shoes went up 73 per cent, of men's shoes 93 per cent. The price of white bread doubled; so did the price of a plow. The price of a semiprivate room in a hospital went up 170 per cent. Round-steak and veal-cutlet prices nearly tripled.

In nearly five of these eight years—from January, 1945 to June 30, 1947, and from September, 1950 to January, 1953—controls had been law. And the curious fact is that after a Republican Congress took the controls off—from 1948 to 1949—the consumer price index actually went down.[1]

Faced with these facts, one worker in a hundred protected his family with a clause in his contract—an escalator clause which would tie his wages to the tail of the price kite.[2] But the other workers whose wages were not hooked to prices had to run as fast as they could just to stay even. Moreover, some of those who were intent on stopping inflation felt

---

[1] The postwar figures (1957–59 = 100); 1945: 62.7; 1946: 68.0; 1947: 77.8; 1948: 83.8; 1949: 83.0; 1950: 83.8; 1951: 90.5; 1952: 92.5.

[2] By June of 1950 approximately 500,000 workers had such clauses; the civilian labor force then totaled approximately 63 million.

that wage escalator clauses tied to the cost-of-living index were themselves inflationary.

Among many measures to restore stability to the dollar, one in particular commended itself: a rejection of a persistent policy of massive deficit spending by the national government—of spending more than the government took in.

I had announced, in a 1952 campaign speech at Peoria, Illinois, that it would be a goal of the new Administration to cut federal spending, to eliminate the budget deficit, and to reduce taxes. Throughout the campaign, to illustrate inflation I had used a length of board (sawed to the breaking point in two places) to represent the buying power of a 1945 dollar. To demonstrate the decline in the dollar between 1945 and 1952, I would break off the first third of the board. To illustrate the decline that was probable with eight more years of Fair Deal policies, I would break off another chunk of the board, ending up with a wooden equivalent of a thirty-three-cent dollar in terms of 1945 values. We expended a large pile of lumber in this lesson, but the point got across.

Whether used in a household, a business, or the federal government, the word "budget" conjures up visions of hard work, tough compromises, and regret—the last because of unnecessary expenditures of earlier years. The making of a federal budget imposes one of the most burdensome problems that confronts reponsible officials. Seldom if ever will a government department recommend a reduction in current expenditures—the demand for more and more sums out of the federal Treasury is incessant and insatiable. Invariably the aggregate of these annual requests far exceeds the amounts projected in income.

Yet the objective of any conscientious budget maker is to balance the budget during the business cycle, and in recent times the federal budget makers have had to keep before their eyes, additionally, the depressing picture of a national debt of appalling size—a debt that they feel, or should feel, the necessity for reducing. Congress, of course, jealously holds on to the purse strings of government, and at first glance it would seem that it could limit spending through the simple expedient of specifying by law the maximum size of the debt. But though the Congress has time and time again enacted laws of this exact import, the effort has had limited effect. When the federal debt nears its legal limit, the Congress passes a new law setting the limit higher. The Congress, as a whole, has never been sufficiently committed to frugality and efficiency, in spite of the vast expenditures required for inescapable costs of government, to withstand pressures of special groups within the body politic and the determination of a few self-seeking political leaders to use the Treasury for furthering personal and party ambitions.

When my Administration took over the reins of government in 1953, there was no one among my immediate associates not dedicated, in principle, to the proposition that both federal expenditures and the public debt must be reduced. We believe this to be vital to the expansion of our economy and the future prosperity of the nation.

We also knew that tax rates were so high, partly because of the requirements of World War II and the Korean conflict, that there was some likelihood of destroying the incentive—and the opportunity—of people to save and invest and create jobs. During the 1952 political campaign I had frequently voiced the hope that tax relief could be accorded within a reasonable time; otherwise, I thought serious results would be experienced.

As we began our studies, many people believed that federal expenditures and the national debt had become so great and accompanying tax rates so high that we faced the distinct possibility of living in a permanently controlled economy. If this situation were allowed to continue indefinitely, the country could not long pretend to be one of private, competitive enterprise; we would be accepting a controlled economy as a permanent feature of our society. The cloud of an unwanted socialism seemed to be, at least faintly, appearing on the economic horizon.

Convinced that only through a free and expanding economy could both our marvelous productivity and political liberty be assuredly sustained, we followed the move to eliminate controls with one that made stark necessity the single guide for budgeted expenditures. It was a back-breaking task.

Naturally, we all expected that the budget we inherited for fiscal year 1954 would once again be out of balance; and so it was, by nearly $10 billion. What we did not previously know was that our predecessors had piled on top of this mountainous debt additional C.O.D. purchases —largely in defense contracts—with no income whatsoever in sight to pay for them upon their arrival, over the next few years. These purchases totaled more than $80 billion—more than all the expenditures of the federal government put together from 1789 through World War I.

The federal government, in Mr. Dodge's words,

> resembled a family that had consistently lived well beyond its means; had undergone five years of severe adversity (related to World War II); had only three times in twenty years provided itself with more income than it had spent; had acquired a debt over four times its yearly income; owed more than a year's income on C.O.D.'s that would have to be paid for on delivery; normally had about one month's living expenses in the bank; had relatively little margin before reaching a fixed limit in its bor-

rowing; faced an impending 10 per cent reduction in its income; and had no immediate plans for changing its habits.

The federal government, of course, could never default on paying its debts; but to meet its I.O.U.'s it would have to mire itself into deeper debt.

In addition to the sorry balance sheet we inherited, we had Republican promises to contend with—the promises of some lawmakers to balance the budget immediately and cut taxes no matter what the result. Representative Dan Reed of upstate New York, for example, filed a bill to reduce individual income taxes and announced his intention as chairman of the House Ways and Means Committee, which examined every piece of tax legislation, to let the excess-profits tax expire on June 30. His plan would cost the federal government $3.5 billion in revenue. Senator Taft, while agreeing to the extension of the excess-profits tax in 1953, was by no means disposed to go along the following year with a budget out of balance.

These facts put the Administration in the middle. I, too, wanted reduced expenditures and balanced budgets, but I could never approve a plan to slash necessary defense spending just to contrast Republican economy with Democratic fiscal irresponsibility. Of course the day of deficits had to come to an end. As I told the Republican Legislative leaders later that year, if the Republicans had to continue deficit spending, "those others" might as well be in charge. But time was needed.

We all knew that given the prior Administration's $78.6 billion budget for expenditures in the 1954 fiscal year (July 1, 1953 to July 1, 1954), there was not much elbow room to work in: $55.6 billion of that budget, or 70 per cent, went for the three major national-security items.[3] Another $14.4 billion went for relatively uncontrollable major programs under existing legislation, such as interest on the national debt, veterans' and agricultural programs, and grants to states for public assistance and unemployment compensation. Only $8.6 billion for other classes of spending was projected—not much in which to find savings sufficient to cancel out a deficit originally estimated at nearly $10 billion.

Recognizing the difficulty, on February 3 Budget Director Dodge, with my approval, sent to the head of every executive-branch agency a memorandum outlining the policy for revising the budget. Every agency was to make a progressive reduction in the number of its employees, to proceed only with construction projects which were clearly essential,

---

[3] Department of Defense (military functions); the Mutual Security Administration; and the Atomic Energy Commission.

and in doing so, "to employ the strictest standards of economy" and to question the necessity for every program.

Persistently but selectively in those first months of 1953 we cut our inherited budget for fiscal year 1954; we scaled down the request for new obligational authority (new appropriations) from $72.9 billion to $63.2 billion and the estimated total expenditures from $78.6 billion to $72.1 billion.

On April 30 I met with the legislative leaders. Describing our study of the problems and costs of national security, I told them it would be impossible for us to arrive at a balanced budget immediately; a too rapid reduction in the budget, I said, would have bad repercussions both at home and abroad. Roger Kyes, Deputy Secretary of Defense, pointed out that to get even this far we had had to make a cut in new appropriations in the military budget by $7 billion, justified only by the hopeful outlook for an early armistice in Korea. The upshot, I said, was a reduction of the deficit from the prior Administration's $9.9 billion to less than $4 billion. (The actual deficit turned out to be $3.1 billion.)

The news astounded and upset Senator Taft. This Administration, he argued heatedly, was spending almost as much as the preceding one, and the result would be either more debt or more taxes, and the certain defeat of Republican candidates in 1954. Two thirds of the Republican Congress, he predicted, would vote to cut the Administration's revised budget, and the Republican Party would be split then and there.

He recognized that the lion's share of the budget went into national security. But the trouble, he asserted, was with the people responsible for the military part of the budget. "I have no confidence whatsoever," he said, "in their judgment or their ability to break away from recommendations they have made in the past. There should be a complete resurvey of all military demands and a reduction all along the line." In an obviously emotional state, he went on to say he had opposed a tax cut this year, but could not do so again next year. "What has happened to the Republican hope," he wanted to know, "to get expenditures under the $70 billion mark at once?"

Foster Dulles, George Humphrey, and Joe Dodge, noting my reaction, jumped in, and each made a small speech. Finally, when they had diplomatically given me time to cool off before answering, I responded to Senator Taft's attack.

Of course, like all others present, I deeply respected Senator Taft's views and his dedication to the nation's welfare, but I could not agree that the country should have, or wanted, a tax cut ahead of a balanced budget or a balanced budget ahead of national security. In answer to Senator Taft I took time to review the international situation and this country's global strategy. I referred to the dangers in Iran and pointed out that Western Europe and the oil of the Middle East must in no circumstances fall to Communism. I reminded him of the alarming news of a new Communist invasion of Laos and the continuing wars in Korea and Vietnam. The important thing, I emphasized, was to take hold of the upward trend in appropriations and bend it down. I did not agree that the proposed budget would ruin Republicans in 1954, and in any event I did not believe that the administration could endanger the security of the United States by proposing an inadequate program. In this matter I felt competent to make a more accurate estimate than he could. "Regardless of consequences," I said, "the nation's military security will take first priority in my calculations."

Senator Taft soon calmed down and apologized; he was very much a man and had become my good friend. Though no one in the room knew the fact at that moment, he was even then living through the last painful months of his life.

The more we studied the financial statement we had inherited, the clearer it became that drastic action was indicated.

I wanted to see a tax reduction. But I wanted even more to stop the deterioration of the currency which had been going on for so many years under unsound fiscal and monetary policies. And, between the Scylla of a deep deficit and the Charybdis of an inadequate military budget, we had to make a start without encountering either.

Since 1930 there had been budget surpluses in only four years: 1930, 1947, 1948, and 1951. I had not promised, and I could not in good conscience produce, a balanced budget which would add fiscal year 1954 to that tiny group of years in the black. But I was determined, if humanly possible, to carry on the fight to conduct a revolution which would reverse the trend of the budgets of the past twenty years. It took us two years to do it, but we did achieve a balanced budget, while at the same time providing adequately for every essential function of government.

No Fear of Conservatism*

Eric F. Goldman

The President's attitude toward specific domestic and foreign problems . . . had its varying aspects. He was, as he frequently remarked, "basically conservative." But it was just as true to say that he was—

---

* Reprinted by permission of Alfred A. Knopf, Inc., from *The Crucial Decade* by Eric F. Goldman. Copyright © 1956 by Eric F. Goldman.

and more so than any president in recent American history—generally nonideological. Eisenhower tended to look for an *ad hoc* solution to a given situation and was willing to listen sympathetically to quite contrasting points of view. If he was inclined to believe that a successful businessman had thereby proved his sagacity, he deeply admired his younger brother Milton ("Milt inherited all the brains in the family"), whose mind had been shaped by years of high New Deal and Fair Deal positions.

Any policy in any field had to stand the test of the President's persistent tendency to react less along the lines of doctrine than according to the human aspects of the problem. The journalist Stewart Alsop has recalled an incident of the 1952 campaign. At first Eisenhower was strongly inclined to make a major issue of what seemed to him the excessively pro-labor attitude of Truman in dealing with a serious steel strike. Before committing himself, he asked to be briefed on the facts and some of his labor advisers explained the demands of the union in terms of what the benefits meant to the men's families in a period of rising prices. Eisenhower's reaction was, "Why maybe they ought to have had more than that," and the steel strike never became an important campaign issue.

Around the President were a group of men who were also "basically conservative," most of them more so than Eisenhower, but they had their own flexibility. All of the principal aides had spent their mature careers learning to operate within a New Deal–Fair Deal society. A number of them had served in specific functions for a Democratic Administration. This was particularly true of Eisenhower's chief adviser on foreign affairs, Secretary of State Dulles, who had worked with the State Department during most of the post–World War II period and who played a part in bringing about the highly untraditional decision to intervene in Korea. The two most influential advisers in domestic and defense matters, Secretary of the Treasury George Humphrey and Secretary of Defense Charles Wilson, were decidedly not businessmen of the 1920's type. They were part of the new, more adaptable managerial class.

In 1948 Wilson, wearied by the struggles between General Motors and the United Automobile Workers, had invented the famous "escalator clause" (tying wages to the cost of living) which labor liked so much and which was important in preserving industrial peace in the following years. In 1947 Humphrey demonstrated a similar flexibility. Facing a coal strike, he and Benjamin Fairless of United States Steel met with John L. Lewis for private talks and brought about a settlement largely on Lewis's terms. Many industrialists and a large section of Congress were indignant but Humphrey defended the move on pragmatic grounds, including the statement that Lewis's demands were largely reasonable. Discussing these episodes, the astute journalist Robert Coughlan has commented that Wilson and Humphrey . . .

> have about as much resemblance to the Republican Big Business-man of the Coolidge–Hoover era as the Indian elephant has to the hairy mammoth – the general outline is the same, but there are vital differences in detail. . . . These two performances were neither 'conservatives' nor 'liberal.' They were, however, practical.

Practical men, headed by an essentially nonideological President, trying to govern a nation with conflicting urges—after the winter of 1953–4 the Administration moved increasingly from the severe conservatism of its early phase. The shift was evident in many ways, but it was clearest of all in the fact that Eisenhower was departing somewhat from his pre–F.D.R. conception of the presidency.

He talked less and less about offending no one in Congress, left fewer major decisions to subordinates, spoke out more frequently on public issues. He was giving the appearance at press conferences that he no longer merely tolerated them but intended to use them to press forward his purposes. Only occasionally did he still remark that he just didn't know about the matter under discussion. No one quite said it but a dozen newsmen now came close to applying to this President Bert Andrews's remark about Harry Truman after the election of 1946: Dwight Eisenhower is becoming President of the United States.

   .   .   .   .

The domestic policies that emerged in 1954 and 1955 represented no sharp break. The Administration kept its businessman tone. Just before the elections of 1954, Secretary of Defense Wilson was at it again with his observation, in discussing unemployment, that "I've always liked bird dogs better than kennel-fed dogs myself—you know one who'll get out and hunt for food rather than sit on his fanny and yell." As late as May 1956 another high Administration official, a deputy assistant to the President, Howard Pyle, was apologizing for his "off-hand comment" that the "right to suffer [by unemployment] is one of the joys of a free economy." Particularly in its policies toward government finance, power, and public resources the Administration continued the lines of its first period to such an extent that the New Dealish had tart words. Which was the more serious corruption? they demanded to know. Mink coats and deep-freezers or disposals of the national forests and utility contracts which could mean millions for a few corporations? And Administration figures were still capable of providing caricatures of the conservative leeriness of welfare expenditures by the federal government. When the Salk polio vaccine was announced on April 12, 1955, the problem arose as to how poor families were to get the protection without having to go through the humiliation of declaring that they could not pay for it. A bill was presented in Congress to have the federal government provide free vaccine for all children. Mrs. Oveta Culp Hobby, Secretary of Health, Education and Welfare, was horrified. The bill was "socialized medicine"—by "the back door."

Yet the shift, however restrained, was on. In late 1954 a White House adviser remarked: "The President's changed, George Humphrey's changed—we've all changed since we came here." Eisenhower was seeing more and more of Dr. Arthur Burns, a Columbia economist and now chairman of the Council of Economic Advisers, who believed that

> it is no longer a matter of serious controversy whether the Government should play a positive role in helping to maintain a high level of economic activity. What we debate nowadays is not the need for controlling business cycles, but rather the nature of governmental action, its timing and its extent.

Humphrey, who had taken Taftite steps to raise interest rates, was encouraging measures that would bring them down. "The first moves," he explained in his pragmatic way, "were to stop price rises and inventory inflation. Then, finding we had credit a little tight, we turned around and loosened it."

In April 1954 Secretary of Agriculture Benson cut the price support of butter from 90 to 75 per cent of parity. The dairy industry was furious but Benson, probably the most dogged free-enterprise man in the Cabinet, indicated he would stand firm. The Secretary of Agriculture was soon summoned to the White House. "Ezra," the President said, "I think maybe we went a mite too far this time." Eisenhower pulled a pad of paper toward him and drew a base and a summit line. He pointed to the bottom line. "This is where we are." Then he tapped the upper line. this is where we eventually want to arrive. But we'll have to go more slowly with our changes—like this." The pencil zig-zagged up the length of the sheet. "This is the way we'll have to go—first this way, then that. But we'll always be headed here"—*here* meaning an agriculture more responsive to the play of market forces.

The threatened depression did not come but the Administration shift continued. The trend is summarized by a comparison of the President's 1953, 1954, and 1955 State of the Union messages. The 1953 document had an unmistakable Taftite tone. By 1955 the nature of the address had changed to one which the *New York Times* correctly characterized as a call "for limited extension of measures along the lines of the New Deal." The new direction was plain in the highway, school, slum-clearance, medical insurance, and widened social security bills sent to Congress. They were decidedly un–New Dealish in the amounts of money called for, some of the methods proposed, and the extent to which the Administration pressed for their passage. But they were also decidedly non-Taftian in their assumption that the federal government had to assume responsibility for broad social needs. So far as amount of expenditure was concerned, the programs would raise federal spending in these categories to an annual level four billion dollars higher than it had been under Truman.

Throughout the shift of his Administration, Eisenhower was feeling his way toward some general statement of the domestic aims of his Presidency. He no longer emphasized "conservatism" alone. He tried "dynamic conservatism," "progressive, dynamic conservatism," "progressive moderation," "moderate progressivism," "positive and progressive." But more and more he adopted a formula along the lines of the one he expressed in December 1954. The Administration, Eisenhower remarked then, "must be liberal when it was talking about the relationship between the Government and the individual, conservative when talking about the national economy and the individual's pocketbook."

Adlai Stevenson met a Chicago press conference and said:

> I have never been sure what progressive moderation means, or was it conservative progressivism? *(Laughter)* I have forgotten, and I am not sure what dynamic moderation or moderate dynamism means. I am not even sure what it means when one says that he is a conservative in fiscal affairs and a liberal in human affairs. I assume what it means is that you will strongly recommend the building of a great many schools to accommodate the needs of our children, but not provide the money. *(Laughter)*

Unquestionably there was something ludicrously muddled about the Administration's efforts to describe itself in its new direction, but the very confusion bespoke the essence of where it was going. Conservative in economic matters and liberal in human affairs—the social gains of the New Deal and the Fair Deal were to be preserved, some extensions would be advocated but for the most part not vigorously pressed, and the whole was to be set within a severe budget consciousness.

Chapter Five

The Opposition of the Present

The election of John F. Kennedy in 1960 spurred the conservatives and particularly the ultra-rightists into organizing activity. "Kennedy is in," wrote the newspaper *Human Events,*

> the fight has just begun . . . . What can you do? 1. Buy Goldwater pins, buttons, bumper strips, and color portraits to identify yourself with all those who want to support Goldwater during the coming "Hundred Days" . . . . 2. Organize a Resistance Movement in your community . . . . Resist Socialism. Resist the "Hundred Days." It is in the American tradition for patriots to call together their friends when a crisis like the Kennedy Revolution confronts the American people.

Within a few years the country was made aware of the myriad organizations committed to opposing New Deal, Fair Deal, and New Frontier programs. The political scene witnessed the resurgence of Republican groups, "educational" organizations, and reactionary movements. The latter group, in particular, frustrated in their attempts to alter the course of American change, were drawn to the conspiracy theory of history. They believed that the ideology of the New Deal had permitted the infiltration of communists into the court system, churches, universities, public schools, health services, and legislative bodies. They further concluded that millions of Americans had been unknowingly "duped" into accepting communist influence.

The conservatives, on the other hand, presented a more reasoned opposition to the New Deal tradition. Arguing against what he called "creeping socialism," the conservative called for broader local power, less government involvement in the economy, limited welfare programs, a balanced budget, and greater participation by the business administrator in the operation of the federal government. A judicious statement along these lines is the first excerpt in this chapter, "The ABC's of Conservatism" by Republican Senator John G. Tower of Texas. Note the parallel between Tower's arguments and those of the Republicans during the New Deal period.

The second piece in this section is excerpted from *Up From Liberalism* by William F. Buckley, Jr., one of the most widely read of intellectual conservatives. Buckley first received public attention with his attack on the ideas taught at his alma mater in a book *God and Man at Yale*. He is a popular television personality, edits the conservative periodical *National Review* and expounds a trenchant anti-liberal point of view. He ran for mayor of New York in 1966 on the Conservative ticket but received a small portion of the popular vote.

The third article is taken from Barry Goldwater's book *The Conscience of a Conservative*. The organizing efforts of the conservatives and especially the ultra-conservatives in the early 1960's paid dividends in the Republican National Convention of 1964. Senator Goldwater of Arizona received the nomination after a struggle in the primaries and token opposition at the Convention. Presenting himself as "a choice, not an echo," Goldwater felt that the 1964 election would pit a genuine conservative against the liberal administrations of Roosevelt, Truman, Kennedy, and Johnson for the first time since Hoover's presidency. In the excerpted part of his book, Goldwater calls for the advancement of the "cause of freedom" by enlarging the domain of state power.

Goldwater's decisive defeat by Lyndon B. Johnson dampened the movement to return government to a pre-depression role. But, the anti-New Dealers viewed the defeat as the opening gun in a new battle between liberalism and conservatism. To this end the conservatives labor to educate the public through books, pamphlets, records, films, and other mass media techniques.

Criticism of the New Deal domestic program and its successors, the Fair Deal, the New Frontier, and the Great Society, has come not only from conservative and ultra-right groups in the contemporary period but from the "New Left," which has attacked these programs as having failed to cope with the inequities of wealth distribution, the power of the military–industrial complex, urban riots, ghettos, discrimination, and the activities of the far right. Although the left is not as well financed or organized, and is not as concerned as the right with formal ideology, it has nevertheless focused the nation's attention on these crucial problems by means of mass demonstrations, publications, and the organization of new issues-oriented groups.

Among the most active of the New Left groups are the Students for a Democratic Society. Organized in 1962, SDS reflects the ideas and aspirations of the socially concerned younger generation now in the colleges and universities. At the founding convention held in Port Huron, Michigan (June 11–15, 1962), an initial statement of objectives was developed which provides insight into the motivation of its members: "We are people of this generation, bred in at least modest comfort, housed now in universities, looking uncomfortably to the world we inherit." Unlike the left of the 1930's, which was essentially concerned with the relationship between intellectual commitment and active involvement, the current left eschews ideology and concentrates on active involvement and participation. An excerpt from the *Port Huron Statement* in this chapter invites comparison with Socialist criticisms, and with the attacks on the New Deal from the right wing of the past and present.

The ABC's of Conservatism (1963)*

Senator John G. Tower

Mr. Ronnie Dugger
The Texas Observer
Austin, Texas

DEAR RONNIE:

I am flattered that the *Texas Observer* has asked me to do something on my fundamental beliefs. In your note to me, asking me to do this piece, you observed that " . . . our readers have so little, substantially, in common with you." However, I am always glad to speak or write under critical, as well as favorable circumstances.

Too, I remember a line from Rudyard Kipling: "They cannot know England who only England know." Perhaps some exposure to an honestly expressed conservative viewpoint may cause some of my liberal friends to take better stock of their own positions.

At the outset, I should note that, too often, the doctrinaire liberal or the doctrinaire conservative tends to state his case in a manner that would convey the impression that he is God, dictating the Ten Commandments to Moses. I'm as guilty of this as anyone.

So, perhaps I should start with a little disarming humility and say that I am aware that I have no monopoly on truth and, although political philosophies are things to which insincere men may, from time to time, repair for the sake of political expediency, I will concede the intellectual honesty of those who might be properly regarded as the real opinion leaders of the liberal movement.

---

* This piece appeared as a letter to the editor in the *Texas Observer* (March 21, 1963), entitled "Some Insight into the Conservative Mentality"; it is reprinted here as it was subsequently published in *Human Events* (April 6, 1963) under the present title. Used with the permission of Senator Tower.

However, it occurs to me that they are possessed of a massive conceit. As the attitude toward people low on the socioeconomic scale on the part of the old Tory Democrats of the last century may have been condescendingly philanthropic, so, too, the attitude of the American twentieth century so-called "liberal" is one that sometimes appears to border on contempt for the ability of people in a society to regulate themselves.

Liberal intellectuals cling to the ancient notion that there must be a ruling elite which uses the coercive authority of the state as a means of ordering the lives and destinies of men, through complete planning of the political, economic, and social processes.

As I see it, the function of government is to preserve order in society—not to order society.

It is no more accurate to caricature the conservative as a bloated, greedy, avaricious money bags, bent on the preservation of privilege and the exploitation of the poor, than it is to caricature the liberal as a bewhiskered, red-eyed, bomb-throwing anarchist.

Assuming that the liberal and the conservative have mutually compatible goals: to wit, the elevation of the whole condition of mankind, the enhancement of the individual dignity of man, consistent with our Judeo-Christian system of ethics, morality and humanity, the difference lies in the approach, the conservative being libertarian, the liberal, essentially egalitarian.

In the eyes of the conservative, the liberal approach, too often, becomes an end unto itself and is, therefore, destructive of the goal. The achievement of complete "equality," and its maintenance, it seems to me, would necessarily require substantial sacrifice of individual liberty and freedom of choice.

It appears to me the liberals are bent on the establishment of a system which would marshal the wealth and resources of the land and redistribute them in the form of welfare benefits and public works. While some liberals may not consciously seek the establishment of a Socialist state in America, I believe that many of the programs they advocate establish a trend in that direction.

In seeking the establishment of a planned economy, the liberal apparently fails to take into consideration the fact that capitalism, or the market-regulated economy, has proved to be the most productive system and has afforded the highest standard of living.

Government planning, as one wise man has observed, is not a mature way to organize an economy. It is unproven; it is educated guess-work at best. Carried to its ultimate, it is necessarily tyrannical in character in that it essentially determines what will be produced and consumed, at what jobs people will work, and what compensations they will receive.

A market-regulated economy preserves the democracy of the market place in which the consumers, by the way they spend their dollars, in effect determine what goods and services will be produced.

A system in which taxes become confiscatory, in which there is extensive government competition with business, or, at its worst, one in which the means of production, distribution, and exchange are nationalized, not only denies a certain amount of freedom of choice, it destroys incentive.

I am aware that conservatives are very often accused of placing property rights before human rights. I deny the allegation and defy the alleger. I consider that the right to own and exploit property for private subsistence, or gain, is an essential human right. It prevents the citizenry from being reduced to a status of complete dependency on the government.

I submit, further, that the honest and consistent conservative has equally high regard for other rights which those of us living in an Anglo-Saxon society have grown to expect, such as freedom of speech, press, assembly, and worship. We believe in elaborate safeguards for the accused and equality in the eyes of the law.

On that last point, was it Anatole France who cynically said, "The law in its majestic equality prohibits the rich man from begging alms and sleeping under bridges, as well as the poor man"? I don't believe this comment could characterize our legal and political system, as the conservative thinks it should be. We do not seek to foster or preserve privilege.

Consistent with our notion that government should preserve order in society and should foster a climate of freedom and growth, we approve such measures as anti-trust laws and other legislation designed to protect the general citizenry against the unscrupulous and the greedy—laws that create a climate of opportunity for all the people, regardless of station or origin. In short, we seek a society in which all men can aspire to be successful and have some reasonable chance of realizing that aspiration.

We, therefore, resent a system of taxation and expenditure that penalizes success and encourages indolence, a regulatory system that will prevent one segment of the society from abusing its economic power—but, at the same time, allow, indeed, even encourage another segment to abuse its power with impunity.

Conservatives cling to the idea that ours is, historically has been and ought to be a classless society—one in which people move freely and without prejudice up and down the socioeconomic ladder. We are righteously, rightfully indignant at those who foment class war for political purposes.

It should be obvious to any but the most ignorant that the best interests of the working man are closely identified with the best interests of the proprietors and managers. Certainly, there are legitimate differences between labor and management on hours, wages, and working conditions. But generally, where a favorable climate for business exists, where business prospers, the working man prospers also.

Too often, the cry is raised that we are "aginners"; we are non-progressive because we oppose programs and proposals which are propounded by the Administration. "What are you *for?*" we are asked.

We are for individual liberty and freedom of choice. We are for a market-regulated economy. We are for the responsibilities of government devolving on those organisms of government that are closest to the people. We therefore oppose that which is destructive of what we are for.

Being in the minority, it is our duty to oppose that which we consider to be conducive to the establishment of dangerous trends. When, and if, we succeed to a majority position, then we will propound our own programs—then it will be the liberals who have to hazard the accusations of obstructivism and negativism.

It is often suggested that we have no alternatives to the proposals of this Administration. Why should we oppose bad proposals with programs and proposals that are less bad? Must there always be alternatives?

Well, Ronnie, that about wraps it up. I've probably left out a great deal that I should have said; but I hope this will give your readers some insight into the conservative mentality. We are not without humane feelings; we love our children; we support humanitarian causes; we give as generously of our time and energies to the betterment of our communities as the liberals do—perhaps more so.

We do not deny that responsibilities for the care of the indigent, the education of our children, and the elevation of the whole state of our society, exist. We simply believe that they should devolve on the individual, the family, the community, the local or state government to the maximum degree possible.

Many thanks to you and the *Texas Observer* for giving me this forum. It is a tribute to your desire to be fair-minded.

Very truly yours,

JOHN G. TOWER

The Economic Assumptions of Liberals (1959)*

William F. Buckley, Jr.

Halfway through the second term of Franklin Roosevelt, New Deal brainbusters began to worry about mounting public concern with the soaring national debt. In those days, the size of the debt was on everyone's mind; indeed, Franklin Roosevelt had won a landslide victory in 1932 on a platform that contained the pledge to hack away at a debt which even under the frugal Mr. Hoover, was thought to have grown to menacing size. At just that moment, an insight came to the rescue. Economists throughout the land were electrified by an alluring theory of debt that had grown out of the new, nationalistic economics of John Maynard Keynes. The ghost of the national debt was finally laid! To depict the intoxicating political effect of the discovery, the artist of the *Washington Times–Herald* drew for the front page of his paper a memorable cartoon. In the center, seated on a throne, was a jubilant F.D.R., cigarette tilted almost vertically, grinning from ear to ear. Dancing about him in a circle, hands clasped, his ecstatic braintrusters sang together the magical incantation, the great emancipating formula: "WE OWE IT TO OURSELVES!"

In five talismanic words the planners had disposed of the problem of deficit spending. Anyone, thence-forward, who worried about an increase in the national debt was simply ignorant of a central insight of modern economics: what do we care how much we—the government—owe, so long as we owe it to ourselves?

There is no room in a brief chapter on the root economic assumptions of Liberalism for technical commentary on such economic *tours de force* as the one about the national debt. I am drawn to the *Times–Herald's* amusing cartoon, and its symbolic significance. A root assumption of the Liberal ideology is that, intellectually, man has come to dominate the economic elements, and that we need only will it, in order to have fair weather all the time. The occasional relapses—for instance the recession of the winter of 1957–1958—is due not so much to absence of economic expertise, as to the inexpertness of Republican technicians. An inexpertness traceable, primarily, to their bewitchment by the antique superstitions.

The accelerability of economic development by force of will (a premise of the Point Four Program) is an article of faith for leading Liberal spokesmen. Mr. Walter Reuther is fond of observing that the

* Pages 138–46 from *Up from Liberalism,* © 1959 by William F. Buckley, Jr.; reprinted by permission of Astor-Honor, Inc., 26 East 42d Street, New York, New York, 10017.

years 1953–1958 (recognize?) were years of an "under-utilization of productive resources"; that had the rate of growth gone forward "dynamically," the gross national product would have been "*140 billion dollars* higher over this period." Though Mr. Reuther relies heavily on a demonology, he does not take the pains to motivate the desire of "big business," "vested interests," "warmongers," and "reactionary politicians" to depress the level of economic activity—at their own expense. One would think no one would work more assiduously than a businessman to implement Mr. Reuther's economic schemes, were it demonstrable that they would raise the national income as dramatically as Mr. Reuther contends.

The point is that economics—which to be sure has always had an uneasy time of it asserting its autonomy as a social science—has become the pliant servant of ideology. For all one knows, Mr. Reuther seriously believes the implementation of his political program would have the salutary economic consequences he describes. But one thing is sure, that even if the program could be demonstrated *not* to have such economic consequences, Mr. Reuther would not modify his politics, any more than the economic stupidity of the collective farm has modified Mao Tse-tung's enthusiasm for it. If ideology calls for a fifteen billion dollar program of public health, the assumption is that the fifteen billion dollars are there—somewhere. It becomes pettifoggery and obstructionism to maintain that the money is *not* "there" in the sense of being readily available and uncommitted. It is reactionary to insist that to produce the money it becomes necessary either to raise the level of economic production, thus increasing tax revenues, raise existing taxes, or inflate the money into existence. Such demurrals, it is easy to see by examining the rhetoric of the heavy spenders, are inadmissible. *What is important is the public health program.*[1]

The salient economic assumptions of Liberalism are socialist. They center around the notion that the economic ass can be driven to Point A most speedily by the judicious use of carrot-and-stick, an approach that supersedes the traditional notion of conservatives and classical liberals that we are not to begin with dealing with asses, and that Point A cannot possibly, in a free society, be presumed to be the desired objective of tens of millions of individual human beings.

The Liberal sees no moral problem whatever in divesting the people of that portion of their property necessary to finance the projects

---

[1] Senator William Proxmire of Wisconsin introduced bills in the first four months of 1958 which if passed, analyzed Representative John W. Byrnes (*Congressional Record*, May 8, 1958), would have added 12 billion dollars annually to the federal deficit.

certified by ideology as beneficial to the Whole. Mr. J. K. Galbraith wages total war against any putative right of the individual to decide for himself how to allocate his resources. The typical Liberal will go to considerable pains to avoid having to say, in as many words, that the people don't know what's good for them (the people are not to be thus affronted); and so the new line is that the people, in expressing themselves at the marketplace, are not expressing their own views, but bending to the will of Madison Avenue. "The conventional wisdom," Mr. Galbraith writes,[2]

> holds that the community . . . makes a decision as to how much it will devote to its public services . . . [that the] people decide how much of their private income and goods they will surrender in order to have public services of which they are in greater need. . . . It will be obvious, however, that this view depends on the notion of independently determined consumer wants. . . . But . . . the consumer makes no such choice. He is subject to the forces of advertising and emulation by which production creates its own demand. Advertising operates exclusively, and emulation mainly, . . . on behalf of privately produced goods and services.

And then there is the notorious ingratitude of man, toward the nobleman who has the courage to tell him what he really wants.

> The scientist or engineer or advertising man who devotes himself to developing a new carburetor, cleanser, or depilatory for which the public recognizes no need and will feel none until an advertising campaign arouses it, is one of the valued members of our society. A politician or a public servant who dreams up a new public service is a wastrel. Few public offenses are more reprehensible.[3]

I do not know the name of, and hence am not in a position to lionize, any carburetor-maker, nor do I know the name of a single maker of depilatories (through I am grateful to them all), and surely all the Henry Fords of history do not command the public adulation of a Franklin Roosevelt. No, Mr. Galbraith, it is more nearly the other way 'round: the scientist who develops a new cleanser is likely to find that there is little he can expect in the way of public recognition; and that the financial gain he thought he was at the very least entitled to

---

[2] Definition: That which is thought to be wise by people who disagree with Mr. Galbraith, and isn't. My definition, to be sure, is a paraphrase. For Mr. Galbraith's statement of it, see *The Affluent Society* (Boston: Houghton Mifflin Co., 1958), Chapter II.

[3] *Op. cit.*, p. 203 (English edition). Mr. Galbraith is a classic example of the Liberal-intellectual who sees himself immersed, head barely above water, in the running seas of Philistia. His thesis is nonsense, of course.

has been preempted—somebody got there first, namely, the politician or public servant, who, scoring yet another public success, has just sold the people yet another public service that has to be paid for.

The Liberals' answer? Tax, to preserve the "social balance." And take public spending out of the hands of the people. Institutionalize your tax system. To avoid having to make the difficult public case for public expenditures year after year we might devise a "system of taxation which automatically makes a *pro rata* share of increasing income available to public authority for public purposes."[4]

There once was a moral problem involved in taxation.

No longer. On the contrary, it is clear that to the extent morality figures at all in taxation, it is as an affirmative imperative. It is morally *necessary* to take from the rich, not merely to give to the poor. If there were no poor, it would still be necessary to take from the rich, egalitarianism being a primary goal of the Liberal ideology. In the past generation the concept of private property metamorphosed from a "right" to an instrumental convenience—a long journey from when Aristotle listed "possession" as the tenth "predicament" of the human being. "Probably majority opinion agrees with our own national policy," writes the author of a widely used freshman economics text about the corollary of private property, freedom of enterprise, "that the right of a man to engage in business for himself is not a basic freedom, like freedom from fear [!], and want [!], freedom of speech and of worship."[5]

And so the way is cleared to set up the problem: either the individual disposes of his surplus funds—in which case you have stagnation, chaos, dissipation, incoherence, synthetized desires; or else a central intelligence disposes of it—in which case you have order, progress, social balance, coherence. Looked at in this way, the problem ceases to be "Can the people afford to look after their own health, build their own schools, buy their own homes?" and becomes "Does it not make more sense for political governors to allocate the people's resources as between doctors, schools, and homes, to impose order upon the chaotic and capricious allocation of dollars when left to their owners to spend?"

It is not easy to understand the Liberals' fear of the voluntary approach to society, manifested at so many levels, most recently and most conspicuously in the concerted Liberal opposition to right-to-work laws in the individual states. Their case is not built on the administrative need for one-hundred per cent cooperation. It does not matter

---

[4] *Ibid.*, p. 243.

[5] Theodore Morgan, *Income and Employment* (New York: Prentice Hall, 1947), p. 175. [Exclamation points are Buckley's.]

that a program of federal social security might work just as well if enrollment in it were voluntary. If it *were* voluntary, a presumptive majority would still subscribe (I say that because a law that is on the books in a democratic society is presumed to have the majority's support); and, that being so, the secession of a minority would not alter the economic balances the program presupposes.

But as with joining a union, membership must be compulsory. The reasons are sometimes given that the individual cannot be trusted to set aside savings toward his old age, and a government cannot very well address the delinquent, arriving, destitute, at old age, as the ant addressed the grasshopper, refusing him sustenance in the name of abstract justice. But has any Liberal suggested that in deference to the ideal of free choice an individual be exempted from membership in the social security program if he *has* taken substitute measures to look after his old age, through the use of private pension schemes, investment or insurance programs?

Although they represent only ten per cent of the whole, and are constantly defending themselves against the attacks of secularists and levellers, the private grammar and secondary schools in this country flourish, and operate under the voluntarist dispensation. "Education" is compulsory. Educational facilities are publicly provided. But those who elect to do so, and can afford to, may seek out private educational facilities. The arrangement is a very ancient one, and is secured by the prescriptive sanction of the public. But private schools remain an anomaly of the planned society; they are "divisive" and "undemocratic," in the words of Dr. James Conant, who spoke as president of the most venerable private educational institution in the land, and so are subject to indirect and direct harassments. The former consist primarily in steeply progressive income taxes. The latter in such measures as educational anti-discrimination laws, and petty refusals to provide milk and buses, under the pretext that to do so would make the authors of the First Amendment roll about in their graves. "The American people are so enamored of equality," De Tocqueville wrote, "that they would rather be equal in slavery than unequal in freedom."

The call by Liberalism to conformity with its economic dispensations does not grow out of the economic requirements of modern life; but rather out of Liberalism's total appetite for power. The root assumptions of Liberal economic theory are that there is no serious economic problem; that in any case economic considerations cannot be permitted to stand in the way of "progress"; that, economically speaking, the people are merely gatherers of money which it is the right and duty of a central intelligence to distribute.

States' Rights (1960)*

Senator Barry Goldwater

The Governor of New York in 1930, pointed out that the Constitution does not empower the Congress to deal with "a great number of . . . vital problems of government, such as the conduct of public utilities, of banks, of insurance, of business, of agriculture, of education, of social welfare, and a dozen other important features." And he added that "Washington must not be encouraged to interfere" in these areas.

Franklin Roosevelt's rapid conversion from Constitutionalism to the doctrine of unlimited government, is an oft-told story. But I am here concerned not so much by the abandonment of States' Rights by the national Democratic Party—an event that occurred some years ago when that party was captured by the Socialist ideologues in and about the labor movement—as by the unmistakable tendency of the Republican Party to adopt the same course. The result is that today *neither* of our two parties maintains a meaningful commitment to the principle of States' Rights. Thus, the cornerstone of the Republic, our chief bulwark against the encroachment of individual freedom by Big Government, is fast disappearing under the piling sands of absolutism.

The Republican Party, to be sure, gives lip-service to States' Rights. We often *talk* about "returning to the States their rightful powers"; the Administration has even gone so far as to sponsor a federal–state conference on the problem. But deeds are what count, and I regret to say that in actual practice, the Republican Party, like the Democratic Party, summons the coercive power of the federal government whenever national leaders conclude that the States are not performing satisfactorily.

Let us focus attention on one method of federal interference—one that tends to be neglected in much of the public discussion of the problem. In recent years the federal government has continued, and in many cases has increased, federal "grants-in-aid" to the States in a number of areas in which the Constitution recognizes the exclusive jurisdiction of the States. These grants are called "matching funds" and are designed to "stimulate" state spending in health, education, welfare, conservation or any other area in which the federal government decides there is a need for national action. If the States agree to put up money for these purposes, the federal government undertakes to match the appropriation according to a ratio prescribed by Congress.

* From Chapter Three by the same title in Barry Goldwater, *The Conscience of a Conservative* (Shepardsville, Kentucky: Victor Publishing Co., 1960), pp. 24–7, 29–30.

Sometimes the ratio is fifty–fifty; often the federal government contributes over half the cost.

There are two things to note about these programs. The first is that they are *federal* programs—they are conceived by the federal government both as to purpose and as to extent. The second is that the "stimulative" grants are, in effect, a mixture of blackmail and bribery. The States are told to go along with the program "or else." Once the federal government has offered matching funds, it is unlikely, as a practical matter, that a member of a State Legislature will turn down his State's fair share of revenue collected from all of the States. Understandably, many legislators feel that to refuse aid would be political suicide. This is an indirect form of coercion, but it is effective nonetheless.

A more direct method of coercion is for the federal government to *threaten* to move in unless state governments take action that Washington deems appropriate. Not so long ago, for example, the Secretary of Labor gave the States a lecture on the wisdom of enacting "up-to-date" unemployment compensation laws. He made no effort to disguise the alternative: if the States failed to act, the federal government would.

Here are some examples of the "stimulative" approach. Late in 1957 a "Joint Federal–State Action Committee" recommended that certain matching funds programs be "returned" to the States on the scarcely disguised grounds that the States, in the view of the Committee, had learned to live up to their responsibilities. These are the areas in which the States were learning to behave: "vocational education" programs in agriculture, home economics, practical nursing, and the fisheries trade; local sewage projects; slum clearance and urban renewal; and enforcement of health and safety standards in connection with the atomic energy program.

Now the point is not that Congress failed to act on these recommendations, or that the Administration gave them only half-hearted support; but rather that the federal government had no business entering these fields in the first place, and thus had no business taking upon itself the prerogative of judging the States' performance. The Republican Party should have said this plainly and forthrightly and demanded the immediate withdrawal of the federal government.

.   .   .   .

But again, I caution against a defensive, or apologetic, appeal to the Constitution. There is a *reason* for its reservation of States' Rights. Not only does it prevent the accumulation of power in a central government that is remote from the people and relatively immune from popular restraints; it also recognizes the principle that essentially local problems are best dealt with by the people most directly concerned. Who knows better than New Yorkers how much and what kind of publicly-financed slum clearance in New York City is needed and can be afforded? Who knows better than Nebraskans whether that State has an adequate nursing program? Who knows better than Arizonans the kind of school program that is needed to educate their children? The people of my own State—and I am confidant that I speak for the majority of them—have long since seen through the spurious suggestion that federal aid comes "free." They know that the money comes out of their own pockets, and that it is returned to them minus a broker's fee taken by the federal bureaucracy. They know, too, that the power to decide how that money shall be spent is withdrawn from them and exercised by some planning board deep in the caverns of one of the federal agencies. They understand this represents a great and perhaps irreparable loss—not only in their wealth, but in their priceless liberty.

Nothing could so far advance the cause of freedom as for state officials throughout the land to assert their rightful claims to lost state officials throughout the land to assert their rightful claims to lost state power; and for the federal government to withdraw promptly and totally from every jurisdiction which the Constitution reserved to the states.

The Remote Control Economy (1962)*

Introductory note: —The following document, the *Port Huron Statement*, was the first official statement of Students for a Democratic Society. The *Statement* represents the collective thought of the founding Convention of SDS, held in Port Huron, Michigan, June 11–15, 1962.

At the time of its writing, the Convention declared the *Port Huron Statement* to be "a living document open to change with our times and experience." Since its adoption there have been changes in the American and world scenes, and changes in SDS as well. And although few of its original writers would agree today with all of its conclusions, it remains

---

* From *The Port Huron Statement* (Chicago: Students for a Democratic Society, 1966), pp. 14–23. Used with permission of SDS.

an essential of SDS direction, a continual stimulus to thinking on campuses and in the movement, and one of the earliest embodiments of the feelings of the new movement of young people which began in the sixties. It should, however, be considered as an historical document, not as a reflection of the present views or politics of SDS.

. . . .

American capitalism today advertises itself as the Welfare State. Many of us comfortably expect pensions, medical care, unemployment compensation, and other social services in our lifetimes. Even with one-fourth of our productive capacity unused, the majority of Americans are living in relative comfort—although their nagging incentive to "keep up" makes them continually dissatisfied with their possessions. In many places, unrestrained bosses, uncontrolled machines, and sweatshop conditions have been reformed or abolished and suffering tremendously relieved. But in spite of the benign yet obscuring effects of the New Deal reforms and the reassuring phrases of government economists and politicians, the paradoxes and myths of the economy are sufficient to irritate our complacency and reveal to us some essential causes of the American malaise.

We live amidst a national celebration of economic prosperity while poverty and deprivation remain an unbreakable way of life for millions in the "affluent society," including many of our own generation. We hear glib references to the "welfare state," "free enterprise," and "share-holder's democracy" while military defense is the main item of "public" spending and obvious oligopoly and other forms of minority rule defy real individual initiative or popular control. Work, too, is often unfulfilling and victimizing, accepted as a channel to status or plenty, if not a way to pay the bills, rarely as a means of understanding and controlling self and events. In work and leisure the individual is regulated as part of the system, a consuming unit, bombarded by hard-sell, soft-sell, lies and semi-true appeals to his basest drives. He is always told that he is a "free" man because of "free enterprise."

The Remote Control Economy

We are subject to a remote control economy, which excludes the mass of individual "units"—the people—from basic decisions affecting the nature and organization of work, rewards, and opportunities. The modern concentration of wealth is fantastic. The wealthiest one per cent of Americans own more than 80 per cent of all personal shares of stock.[1] From World War II until the mid-fifties, the 50 biggest corporations increased their manufacturing production from 17 to 23 per cent of the national total, and the share of the largest 200 companies rose from 30 to 37 per cent. To regard the various decisions of these elites as purely economic is short-sighted: their decisions affect in a momentous way the entire fabric of social life in America. Foreign investments influence political policies in underdeveloped areas—and our efforts to build a "profitable" capitalist world blind our foreign policy to mankind's needs and destiny. The drive for sales spurs phenomenal advertising efforts; the ethical drug industry, for instance, spent more than $750 million on promotions in 1960, nearly four times the amount available to all American medical schools for their educational programs. The arts, too, are organized substantially according to their commercial appeal; aesthetic values are subordinated to exchange values, and writers swiftly learn to consider the commercial market as much as the humanistic marketplace of ideas. The tendency to over-production, to gluts of surplus commodities, encourages "market research" techniques to deliberately create pseudo-needs in consumers—we learn to buy "smart" things, regardless of their utility— and introduces wasteful "planned obsolescence" as a permanent feature of business strategy. While real social needs accumulate as rapidly as profits, it becomes evident that Money, instead of dignity of character, remains a pivotal American value and Profitability, instead of social use, a pivotal standard in determining priorities of resource allocation.

Within existing arrangements, the American business community cannot be said to encourage a democratic process nationally. Economic minorities not responsible to a public in any democratic fashion make decisions of a more profound importance than even those made by Congress. Such a claim is usually dismissed by respectful and knowing citations of the ways in which government asserts itself as keeper of the public interest at times of business irresponsibility. But the real,

---

[1] Statistics on wealth reveal the "have" and "have not" gap at home. Only 5 per cent of all those in the $5,000 or less bracket own any stock at all. In 1953, personally-owned wealth in the U.S. stood at $1 trillion. Of this sum, $309.2 billion (30.2 per cent) was owned by 1,659,000 top wealth-holders (with incomes of $60,000 or more). This elite comprised 1.04 per cent of the population. Their average gross estate estimate was $182,000, as against the national average of $10,000. They held 80 per cent of all corporation stock, virtually all state and local bonds, and between 10 and 33 per cent of other types of property: bonds, real estate, mortgages, life insurance, unincorporated businesses, and cash. They receive 40 per cent of property, income-rent, interest dividends. The size of this elite's wealth has been relatively constant: 31.6% (1922), 30.6% (1939), 29.8% (1949), 30.2% (1958).

as opposed to the mythical, range of government "control" of the economy includes only:

1) some limited "regulatory" powers—which usually just ratify industry policies or serve as palliatives at the margins of significant business activity;

2) a fiscal policy built upon defense expenditures as pump-priming "public works"—without a significant emphasis on peaceful "public works" to meet social priorities and alleviate personal hardships;

3) limited fiscal and monetary weapons which are rigid and have only minor effects, and are greatly limited by corporate veto: tax cuts and reforms; interest rate control (used generally to tug on investment but hurting the little investor most); tariffs which protect non-competitive industries with political power and which keep less-favored nations out of the large trade mainstream, as the removal of barriers reciprocally with the Common Market may do disastrously to emerging countries outside of Europe: wage arbitration, the use of government coercion in the name of "public interest" to hide the tensions between workers and business production controllers; price controls, which further maintain the status quo of big ownership and flushes out little investors for the sake of "stability";

4) very limited "poverty-solving" which is designed for the organized working class but not the shut-out, poverty-stricken migrants, farm workers, the indigent unaware of medical care or the lower-middle class person riddled with medical bills, the "unhireables" or minority groups or workers over 45 years of age, etc.;

5) regional development programs—such as the Area Redevelopment Act—which have been only "trickle down" welfare programs without broad authority for regional planning and development and public works spending. The federal highway program has been more significant than the "depressed areas" program in meeting the needs of people, but it is generally too remote and does not reach the vicious circle of poverty itself.

In short, the theory of government's "countervailing" business neglects the extent to which government influence is marginal to the basic production decisions, the basic decision-making environment of society, the basic structure of distribution and allocation which is still determined by major corporations with power and wealth concentrated among the few. A conscious conspiracy—as in the case of price-rigging in the electrical industry—is by no means generally or continuously operative but power undeniably does rest in comparative insulation from the public and its political representatives.

The Military–Industrial Complex

The most spectacular and important creation of the authoritarian and oligopolistic structure of economic decision-making in America is the institution called "the military–industrial complex" by former President Eisenhower—the powerful congruence of interest and structure among military and business elites which affects so much of our development and destiny. Not only is ours the first generation to live with the possibility of world-wide cataclysm—it is the first to experience the actual social preparation for cataclysm, the general militarization of American society. In 1948 Congress established Universal Military Training, the first peacetime conscription. The military became a permanent institution. Four years earlier, General Motors' Charles E. Wilson had heralded the creation of what he called the "permanent war economy," the continuous use of military spending as a solution of economic problems unsolved before the post-war boom, most notably the problem of the seventeen million jobless after eight years of the New Deal. This has left a "hidden crisis" in the allocation of resources by the American economy.

Since our childhood these two trends—the rise of the military and the installation of a defense-based economy—have grown fantastically. The Department of Defense, ironically the world's largest single organization, is worth $160 billion, owns 32 million acres of America and employs half the 7.5 million persons directly dependent on the military for subsistence, has an $11 billion payroll which is larger than the net annual income of all American corporations. Defense spending in the Eisenhower era totaled $350 billions and President Kennedy entered office pledged to go even beyond the present defense allocation of 60 cents from every public dollar spent. Except for a war-induced boom immediately after "our side" bombed Hiroshima, American economic prosperity has coincided with a growing dependence on military outlay—from 1941 to 1959 America's Gross National Product of $5.25 trillion included $700 billion in goods and services purchased for the defense effort, about one-seventh of the accumulated GNP. This pattern has included the steady concentration of military spending among a few corporations. In 1961, 86 per cent of Defense Department contracts were awarded without competition. The ordnance industry of 100,000 people is completely engaged in military work; in the aircraft industry, 94 per cent of 750,000 workers are linked to the war economy; shipbuilding, radio and communications equipment industries commit 40 per cent of their work to defense; iron and steel, petroleum, metal-stamping and machine shop products, motors and generators, tools and hardware, copper, aluminum, and machine tools industries all devote at least 10 per cent of their work to the same cause.

The intermingling of Big Military and Big Industry is evidenced in the 1,400 former officers working for the 100 corporations who received nearly all the $21 billion spent in procurement by the Defense Department in 1961. The overlap is most poignantly clear in the case of General Dynamics, the company which received the best 1961 contracts, employed the most retired officers (187), and is directed by a former Secretary of the Army. A *Fortune* magazine profile of General Dynamics said: "The unique group of men who run Dynamics are only incidentally in rivalry with other U.S. manufacturers, with many of whom they actually act in concert. Their chief competitor is the USSR. The core of General Dynamics' corporate philosophy is the conviction that national defense is a more or less permament business." Little has changed since Wilson's proud declaration of the Permanent War Economy back in the 1944 days when the top 200 corporations possessed 80 per cent of all active prime war-supply contracts.

Military–Industrial Politics

The military and its supporting business foundation have found numerous forms of political expression, and we have heard their din endlessly. There has not been a major Congressional split on the issue of continued defense spending spirals in our lifetime. The triangular relations of the business, military, and political arenas cannot be better expressed than in Dixiecrat Carl Vinson's remarks as his House Armed Services Committee reported out a military construction bill of $808 million throughout the fifty states, for 1960–61: "There is something in this bill for everyone," he announced. President Kennedy had earlier acknowledged the valuable anti-recession features of the bill.

Imagine, on the other hand, $808 million suggested as an anti-recession measure, but being poured into programs of social welfare: the impossibility of receiving support for such a measure identifies a crucial feature of defense spending—it is beneficial to private enterprise, while welfare spending is not. Defense spending does not "compete" with the private sector; it contains a natural obsolescence; its "confidential" nature permits easier boondoggling; the tax burdens to which it leads can be shunted from corporation to consumer as a "cost of production." Welfare spending, however, involves the government in competition with private corporations and contractors; it conflicts with immediate interests of private pressure groups; it leads to taxes on business. Think of the opposition of private power companies to current proposals for river and valley development, or the hostility of the real estate lobby to urban renewal; or the attitude of the American Medical Association to a paltry medical care bill; or of all business lobbyists to foreign aid; these are the pressures leading to the schizophrenic public–military, private–civilian economy of our epoch. The politicians, of course, take the line of least resistance and thickest support: warfare, instead of welfare, is easiest to stand up for: after all, the Free World is at stake (and our constituency's investments, too.)

Automation, Abundance, and Challenge

But while the economy remains relatively static in its setting of priorities and allocation of resources, new conditions are emerging with enormous implications: the revolution of automation, and the replacement of scarcity by the potential of material abundance.

Automation, the process of machines replacing men in performing sensory, motoric, and complex logical tasks, is transforming society in ways that are scarcely comprehensible. By 1959, industrial production regained its 1957 "pre-recession" level—but with 750,000 fewer workers required. In the fifties as a whole, national production enlarged by 43 per cent but the number of factory employees remained stationary, seven-tenths of one per cent higher than in 1947.[2] Automation is destroying whole categories of work—impersonal thinkers have efficiently labeled this "structural unemployment"—in blue-collar, service, and even middle-management occupations. In addition it is eliminating employment opportunities for a youth force that numbers one million more than it did in 1950, and rendering work far more difficult both to find and do for people in their forties and up. The consequences of this economic drama, strengthened by the force of post-war recessions,

---

[2] The electronics industry lost 200,000 of 900,000 workers in the years 1953–57. In the steel industry, productive capacity has increased 20 per cent since 1955, while the number of workers has fallen 17,000. Employment in the auto industry decreased in the same period from 746,000 to 614,000. The chemical industry has enlarged its productive powers 27 per cent although its work force has dropped by 3 per cent. A farmer in 1962 can grow enough to feed 24 people, where one generation ago only 12 could be nourished. The United States Bureau of the Census used 50 statisticians in 1960 to perform the service that required 4,100 in 1950.

are momentous: five million becomes an acceptable unemployment tabulation, and misery, uprootedness, and anxiety become the lot of increasing numbers of Americans.

But while automation is creating social dislocation of a stunning kind, it paradoxically is imparting the opportunity for men the world around to rise in dignity from their knees. The dominant optimistic economic fact of this epoch is that fewer hands are needed now in actual production, although more goods and services are a real potentiality. The world could be fed, poverty abolished, the great public needs could be met, the brutish world of Darwinian scarcity could be brushed away, all men could have more time to pursue their leisure, drudgery in work could be cut to a minimum, education could become more of a continuing process for all people, both public and personal needs could be met rationally. But only in a system with selfish production motives and elitist control, a system which is less welfare- than war-based, undemocratic rather than "stock-holder participative" as "sold to us," does the potentiality for abundance become a curse and a cruel irony:

1) Automation brings unemployment instead of more leisure for all and greater achievement of needs for all people in the world—a crisis instead of economic utopia. Instead of being introduced into a social system in a planned and equitable way, automation is initiated according to its profitability. The American Telephone and Telegraph holds back modern telephone equipment, invented with public research funds, until present equipment is *financially* unprofitable. Colleges develop teaching machines, mass-class techniques, and TV education to replace teachers: not to proliferate knowledge or to assist the qualified professors now, but . . . [typographical confusion in original]. Technology, which could be a blessing to society, becomes more and more a sinister threat to humanistic and rational enterprise.

2) Hard-core poverty exists just beyond the neon lights of affluence, and the "have-nots" may be driven still further from opportunity as the high-technology society demands better education to get into the production mainstream and more capital investment to get into "business." Poverty is shameful in that it herds people by race, religion, and previous condition of misfortune into "uneconomic classes" in the so-called free society— the marginal worker is made more insecure by automation, high education requirements, heavier competition

for jobs, the maintenance of low wages, and a high level of unemployment. People in the rut of poverty are strikingly unable to overcome the collection of forces working against them: poor health, bad neighborhoods, miserable schools, inadequate "welfare" services, unemployment and underemployment, weak political and union organization.

3) Surplus and potential plenty are wasted domestically and producers suffer impoverishment because the real needs of the world and of our society are not reflected in the market. Our huge bins of decomposing grain are classic American examples, as is the steel industry which, in the summer of 1962, is producing at 53 per cent of capacity.

The Stance of Labor

Amidst all this, what of organized labor, the historic institutional representative of the exploited, the presumed "countervailing power" against the excesses of Big Business? The contemporary social assault on the labor movement is of crisis proportions. To the average American, "big labor" is a growing cancer equal in impact to Big Business—nothing could be more distorted, even granting a sizeable union bureaucracy. But in addition to public exaggerations, the labor crisis can be measured in several ways. First, the high expectations of the newborn AFL–CIO of 30 million members by 1965 are suffering a reverse unimaginable five years ago. The demise of the dream of "organizing the unorganized" is dramatically reflected in the AFL–CIO decision, just two years after its creation, to slash its organizing staff in half. From 15 million members when the AFL and CIO merged, the total has slipped to 13.5 million. During the post-war generation, union membership nationally has increased by four million—but the total number of workers has jumped by 13 million. Today only 40 per cent of all non-agricultural workers are protected by any form of organization. Second, organizing conditions are going to worsen. Where labor now is strongest—in industries—automation is leading to an attrition of available work. As the number of jobs dwindles, so does labor's power of bargaining, since management can handle a strike in an automated plant more easily than the older mass-operated ones.

More important, perhaps, the American economy has changed radically in the last decade, as suddenly the number of workers producing goods became fewer than the number in "nonproductive" areas —government, trade, finance, services, utilities, transportation. Since

World War II "white collar" and "service" jobs have grown twice as fast as have "blue collar" production jobs. Labor has almost no organization in the expanding occupational areas of the new economy, but almost all of its entrenched strength in contracting areas. As big government hires more, as business seeks more office workers and skilled technicians, and as growing commercial America demands new hotels, service stations and the like, the conditions will become graver still. Further, there is continuing hostility to labor by the Southern states and their industrial interests—meaning "runaway" plants, cheap labor threatening the organized trade union movement, and opposition from Dixecrats to favorable labor legislation in Congress. Finally, there is indication that Big Business, for the sake of public relations if nothing more, has acknowledged labor's "right" to exist, but has deliberately tried to contain labor at its present strength, preventing strong unions from helping weaker ones or from spreading to unorganized sectors of the economy. Business is aided in its efforts by proliferation of "right-to-work" laws at state levels (especially in areas where labor is without organizing strength to begin with), and anti-labor legislation in Congress.

In the midst of these besetting crises, labor itself faces its own problems of vision and program. Historically, there can be no doubt as to its worth in American politics—what progress there has been in meeting human needs in this century rests greatly with the labor movement. And to a considerable extent the social democracy for which labor has fought externally is reflected in its own essentially democratic character: representing millions of people, not millions of dollars; demanding their welfare, not eternal profit.

Today labor remains the most liberal "mainstream" instutition— but often its liberalism represents vestigial commitments, self-interestedness, unradicalism. In some measure labor has succumbed to institutionalization, its social idealism waning under the tendencies of bureaucracy, materialism, business ethics. The successes of the last generation perhaps have braked, rather than accelerated labor's zeal for change. Even the House of Labor has bay windows: not only is this true of the labor elites, but as well of some of the rank-and-file. Many of the latter are indifferent unionists, uninterested in meetings, alienated from the complexities of the labor-management negotiating apparatus, lulled to comfort by the accessibility of luxury and the opportunity of long-term contracts. "Union democracy" is not simply inhibited by labor-leader elitism, but by the related problem of rank-and-file apathy to the tradition of unionism. The crisis of labor is reflected in the co-existence within the unions of militant Negro discontents and discriminatory locals, sweeping critics of the obscuring "public interest" marginal tinkering of government and willing handmaidens of conservative political leadership, austere sacrificers and business-like operators, visionaries and anachronisms—tensions between extremes that keep alive the possibilities for a more militant unionism. Too, there are seeds of rebirth in the "organizational crisis" itself: the technologically unemployed, the unorganized white collar men and women, the migrants and farm workers, the unprotected Negroes, the poor, all of whom are isolated now from the power structure of the economy, but who are the potential base for a broader and more forceful unionism.

Horizon

In summary: a more reformed, more human capitalism, functioning at three-fourths capacity while one-third of America and two-thirds of the world goes needy, domination of politics and the economy by fantastically rich elites, accommodation and limited effectiveness by the labor movement, hard-core poverty and unemployment, automation confirming the dark ascension of machine over man instead of shared abundance, technological change being introduced into the economy by the criteria of profitably—this has been our inheritance. However inadequate, it has instilled quiescence in liberal hearts— partly reflecting the extent to which misery has been overcome, but also the eclipse of social ideals. Though many of us are "affluent," poverty, waste, elitism, manipulation are too manifest to go unnoticed, too clearly unnecessary to go accepted. To change the Cold War status quo and other social evils, concern with the challenges to the American economic machine must expand. Now, as a truly better social state becomes visible, a new poverty impends: a poverty of vision, and a poverty of political action to make that vision reality. Without new vision, the failure to achieve our potentialities will spell the inability of our society to endure in a world of obvious, crying needs and rapid change.